EDITOR IN CHIEF®

Book B2 Grammar Disasters and Punctuation Faux Pas

SERIES TITLES:

Editor in Chief® Beginning

Editor in Chief® A1 • Editor in Chief® B1 • Editor in Chief® C1

Editor in Chief® A2 • Editor in Chief® B2 • Editor in Chief® C2

Created by Michael Baker

Written by Carrie Beckwith, Cheryl Block,
Margaret Hockett, & David White

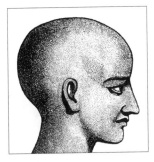

© 1999
CRITICAL THINKING BOOKS & SOFTWARE
www.CriticalThinking.com
P.O. Box 448 • Pacific Grove • CA 93950-0448
Phone 800-458-4849 • FAX 831-393-3277
ISBN 0-89455-720-3
Printed in the United States of America

TABLE OF CONTENTS

TO THE TEACHER

Objective

Editor in Chief® reinforces the rules of written English by providing the student with practice in editing a variety of formats. Students develop a basic understanding of the rules of grammar and mechanics in context and exercise their critical thinking abilities by identifying content errors. Book A covers the skills generally taught in grades 4–6, Book B covers those taught in grades 6–8, and Book C covers skills for grades 8 and up.

Rationale

The key difference between *Editor in Chief*® and most grammar series is the focus on editing in context. The grammatical and mechanical errors inserted into the activities are based on general instructional guidelines for specific grade levels; the content level, however, remains ungraded, allowing usage of these materials at many instructional levels. Styles and content are varied to sustain interest and broaden the student's exposure to different writing formats such as letters, advertisements, and dialogue. The illustrations integrated into the context of the activities further spark student interest. The editing skills developed can be applied to the student's own writing.

Activity

Each activity consists of at least 1 content error (a discrepancy between the illustration/caption and the writing sample) and 9–15 errors in spelling, mechanics, and grammar. The student is asked to identify these errors and make the appropriate corrections. An editing checklist, included on page ix of this book, may be used by the student to aid in the editing task. Most corrections involve the insertion, modification, or deletion of punctuation marks, capitals, and single words within the text. Each writing sample is based on an accompanying illustration and caption. Information in the illustration and caption is correct (content errors occur only where the story is *contradicted* by the illustration or caption). The student may insert corrections and recopy the corrected article on the lines provided. Activities are sequenced according to the type, number, and level of errors included and the complexity of the subject matter.

Book B2 has the same type of errors as Book B1, but the number of errors and the complexity of context has increased.

Using the Answer Key

The answer key beginning on page 34 lists corrections for each article. Each numbered error correction is followed by a short-hand explanation of the error type and a bracketed reference to the specific rules in the Grammar Guide, which begins on page 61. The teacher may choose to provide students with the number and type of errors prior to editing. In some instances, a student may be able to correct an error in more than one way. The answer key gives some obvious choices, but the teacher may choose to accept other answers that make sense and are grammatically and mechanically correct.

Teaching Suggestions

Editor in Chief® can be used as an individual or group activity for instruction, reinforcement, practice, and assessment of English grammar and mechanics. When introducing a new rule, one article can serve as an instructional example and a second as an assessment of students' independent understanding. This book provides an excellent tool for authentic assessment of students' knowledge of grammar and mechanics. The Scope and Sequence on page vii gives teachers an overview of the types of errors included in each article, enabling them to more easily individualize lessons. The Styles and Topics on page viii list the type of writing and the content for each exercise.

Suggested Uses for Editor in Chief®

Regular Usage

- Group instruction—EIC format is ideal for overhead projector.

- Cooperative Learning—Students edit and exchange work to proofread.

- Homework—Individual activities can follow class instruction.

Extension Activities

- Students write their own paragraphs for editing.

- EIC fosters class discussion of writing errors and how to avoid them.

- Checklist can be used to transfer editing skills to other writing activities.

Sources and Standards

In preparing this manuscript, we used the following references as standards for spelling, grammar, punctuation, and usage:

The American Heritage Dictionary, 3rd ed. (Boston: Houghton Mifflin Company, 1993).

The Chicago Manual of Style, 14th ed. (Chicago: The University of Chicago Press, 1993).

The Merriam-Webster Concise Handbook for Writers (Springfield, Mass.: Merriam-Webster Inc, 1991).

The Merriam-Webster Dictionary of English Usage (Springfield, Mass.: Merriam-Webster Inc, 1989).

The New York Public Library Writer's Guide to Style and Usage (New York: HarperCollins Publishers, Inc., 1994).

Warriner's English Grammar and Composition: Complete Course, Liberty Edition (Orlando: Harcourt Brace Jovanovich, 1986).

SCOPE AND SEQUENCE: EDITOR IN CHIEF® BOOK B2

TYPE OF ERROR	1	2	3	4	5	6	7	8	9	10	11	12	13	14	15	16	17	18	19	20	21	22	23	24	25	26	27	28	29	30	31	32	33
GRAMMAR/USAGE																																	
Adjective		■										■																	■				
Adjec: comp./superl.				■		■													■									■		■		■	
Adverb		■	■							■						■		■				■	■										
Adverb: comp./superl.			■																			■	■		■							■	■
Agree: adjec./noun		■											■						■							■							
Agree: subject/verb	■					■	■	■	■	■	■	■	■	■			■	■	■									■	■		■		
Agree: pron./noun	■	■			■								■				■						■		■								
Article: a or an						■											■										■			■			
Conjunction: correlat.		■																													■		
Misplaced modifier																	■							■							■		
Pronoun: subj./object	■		■		■		■	■					■						■				■	■	■	■			■	■	■		
Pronoun: possessive			■										■	■			■			■				■									
Pronoun: reflexive																															■		
Pronoun: first person																											■			■			
Tense: present/past			■	■		■			■			■		■	■								■			■		■					■
Tense: future													■						■						■								
Unnecessary words														■										■									
Verb: participle	■					■	■				■			■	■					■		■	■	■			■						■
Verb: linking, helping									■	■				■	■					■		■	■	■			■						
Word pairs		■			■					■		■														■	■				■		
SPELLING	■					■		■				■	■				■		■			■		■						■			■
PUNCTUATION	1	2	3	4	5	6	7	8	9	10	11	12	13	14	15	16	17	18	19	20	21	22	23	24	25	26	27	28	29	30	31	32	33
Apostrophe: contrac.			■															■											■				
Apostrophe: possess.						■			■		■	■			■						■	■	■				■						
Colon									■				■													■		■					
Comma: series													■					■															
Comma: date/address				■					■		■							■									■		■				
Comma: introductory				■					■	■								■		■		■	■	■	■				■				
Comma: noun of address															■												■						
Comma: interrupter																	■										■						
Comma: appositive							■						■	■					■														
Comma: coordin. conjunction					■											■			■	■											■	■	
Comma: quotation																■			■	■								■	■	■			
Comma: letter		■							■								■							■		■							
Exclamation point																■								■						■		■	
Hyphen				■																■													
Period: declarative						■																				■	■						
Period: abbreviation							■																				■						
Run-on sentence								■		■		■	■	■	■				■														
Sentence fragment	■	■		■		■				■	■					■		■	■		■										■		
Question mark						■												■		■						■		■		■			■
Quotation marks													■			■	■			■							■			■	■		■
CAPITALIZATION	1	2	3	4	5	6	7	8	9	10	11	12	13	14	15	16	17	18	19	20	21	22	23	24	25	26	27	28	29	30	31	32	33
First word of sentence				■																													
Proper noun			■			■	■									■													■				
Proper adjective					■							■																■					
Title/abbreviation			■						■				■							■									■		■		■
In quotations													■								■			■			■		■				
Day, month, holiday				■				■				■																					
Letter: opening, close															■																		

STYLES AND TOPICS: EDITOR IN CHIEF® BOOK B2

EXERCISE TITLE	WRITING STYLE	CONTENT: TOPIC	Fiction/ Nonfiction
1. Do Elephants Mourn?	expository	Science: elephants	nonfiction
2. Up in Arms	narrative (letter)	Job: frustration	fiction
3. Fishy Story	narrative	Adventure: escape	fiction
4. Earth Day Celebration	expository	Ecology: political action	nonfiction
5. The Burning Phoenix	descriptive	Mythology: phoenix	nonfiction
6. The Missing Cookie Caper	narrative	Mystery: theft	fiction
7. America's First Colony	expository	U.S. history: colonial	nonfiction
8. A.S.A.P for the S.P.C.A!	persuasive	Human interest: volunteering	fiction
9. A Foot in the Door	persuasive (letter)	Career: applying for a job	fiction
10. How to Catch a Wave	descriptive	Sports: surfing	nonfiction
11. The Monarch	expository	Science: migration	nonfiction
12. Drumming It In	narrative	Music: percussion	fiction
13. Spiders and Crabs	compare/contrast	Science: arthropods	nonfiction
14. The Giant of His Age	descriptive	Biography: da Vinci	nonfiction
15. Night Fright	narrative	Adventure: practical joke	fiction
16. A Net Gain	narrative	Sports: tennis	fiction
17. A Glimpse into the Past	descriptive (letter)	Geography: Machu Picchu	nonfiction
18. A Sucker for Squid	narrative	Mystery: theft	fiction
19. The Eagle Nebula	expository	Science: nebulae	nonfiction
20. Deadly Dino	descriptive	Natural history: T-rex	nonfiction
21. Victory on Wheels	narrative	Sports: bicycle race	fiction
22. An Archaeological Find	narrative	Archaeology: ring dating	fiction
23. An Early American	narrative/descriptive	Science/History: bison	fiction
24. A Profitable Platform	descriptive (letter)	Politics: student campaign	fiction
25. Heart-Racing Journey	narrative	Science: heart	fiction
26. Schedule It!	narrative	Time management: schedule	fiction
27. Bales of Fun	narrative (letter)	Lifestyle: farming	fiction
28. A Lesson on Haiku	dialog/descriptive	Poetry: haiku	fiction
29. Eclipsed!	expository	Science: solar eclipse	fiction
30. Footnotes in Anatomy	dialog/descriptive	Anatomy: foot	fiction
31. Digits Rule in CD	narrative/descriptive	Technology: CD player	fiction
32. Count on Computers	expository	Math/Technology: base two	nonfiction
33. Animated about Art	narrative/expository	Art/Entertainment: animation	fiction

Editor in Chief®—Editing Checklist

INSTRUCTIONS

The following list gives hints to help you find errors when editing. A word may be misspelled or used incorrectly. Punctuation and capitals may need to be inserted or removed. The caption and picture are always correct, but mistakes have been made in the story. You need to read carefully as you look for errors.

CAPITALIZATION

Are the correct words capitalized? Do other words need capitals?

CONTENT

Does the information in the paragraph match the caption and illustration?

GRAMMAR & USAGE

PUNCTUATION

Adjective or adverb:

What kind of word does it modify? Is the correct form used?

Apostrophe:

Is the word a contraction? Is the word a plural or possessive? Is the apostrophe in the right place?

Agreement:

Does the verb agree with the subject? Does the pronoun agree with the noun it replaces? Does the adjective agree with the noun?

Colon:

Is it used correctly? Is it placed correctly?

Articles:

Do you use "a" or "an"?

Comma:

Is it needed to separate words, dates, phrases, or clauses? Is it placed correctly?

Correlative conjunctions:

Are either/or and neither/nor used correctly?

Exclamation point:

Is it used correctly?

Misplaced modifier:

Does the modifier make sense where it is placed within the sentence?

Hyphen:

Is this a compound number?

Pronoun:

Is it used as a subject or an object? Is the correct form used? Is first person last?

Period:

Is it needed for a sentence or an abbreviation?

Usage:

Is the correct word used? Does a word need to be changed?

Run-on sentence:

Should this be more than one sentence?

Verb tense:

Is the correct form used? Is a helping verb needed?

Sentence fragment:

Is this a complete sentence?

Word pairs that are easily confused:

Is the correct word used?

Question mark:

Is the sentence or quotation a question? Is the question mark placed correctly?

SPELLING

Are the words spelled correctly? Is the plural form correct?

Quotation marks:

Is each part of a divided quotation enclosed? Are other punctuation marks placed correctly inside or outside the quotation marks? Is this a title of a song, chapter, etc.?

1. Do Elephants Mourn?

Do elephants mourn the loss of other elephants? Its a question that has no definite answer, but fascinating behaviors have been observe. Their is documented cases of elephants gathering around the body of a deceased elephant and staying with it for as long as a weak to protect it from scavengers. Seeing the remains of a tusk has prompted some elephants to stop, pick the tusk up with their trunks, caress them, and then pass it among themselves. Some elephants have been observed. Trying to pick up a fallen and wounded elephant with their tails in an attempt to get the fallen elephant to its feet again. Perhaps we will never know if elephants mourn, but it is an interesting question to ponder. What do yourselves think?

Certain behaviors suggest that elephants may have emotions similar to our own. Scientists have observed some elephants using their trunks to help lift fallen and wounded elephants.

Find the 9 errors in this activity. There are no errors in the illustration or the caption.

_____

_____

_____

_____

_____

_____

2. Up in Arms

31 Post Road
Cambridge, MA 02138
August 4, 1999

Dear Kaneesha,

    I was very happy to get the new job, but I have felt like an octopus this last three weeks. It started out easy enough, but then Ms. Atkins piled the work higher and higher. The sketch shows. Me dealing with the usual five phones at a time! I wouldn't mind so much if the boss did some of the work himself. However, she often puts her feet up or even lays down for a nap. She says to me, "Why, you do almost as better a job as I do!" Isn't that awful insulting? Working here is neither fun or profitable, and I could care less for the job. It's time to look for a new one.

Your friend
Johann

Johann imagines himself as an octopus working for Ms. Atkins. Realizing he cared nothing for the job, he sent this sketch and the letter to his friend Kaneesha.

Find the 10 errors in this activity. There are no errors in the illustration or the caption.

_____

_____

_____

_____

_____

_____

3. Fishy Story

I had been diving in the south pacific and studying the local sea life. I'm afraid I come a bit closer to a certain form of sea life than I truly desired. Lets call her Wanda. Though I moved the fast I have ever moved, I could not escape the gaping jaws. Thirtyfour teeth then surrounded me, and them threatened to clamp down harder at any moment. My snorkeling gear seemed to be squeezing my head most tightly than ever. Mine arms were just about to give out. Fortunately, captain Gormand appeared and came quick to my rescue. He was able to prop Wanda's mouth open with a long beam while I escaped. Wanda is probably now telling her friends about the one that got away!

Gerald Carter of London was picked up by Captain Chris Drake, who was sailing alone off the eastern coast of Australia. Carter was shaken, but he was relieved to be free of Wanda's jaws.

Find the 12 errors in this activity. There are no errors in the illustration or the caption.

_____

_____

_____

_____

_____

_____

4. Earth Day Celebration

Earth Day was first celebrated on april 22, 1970 as a nationwide street demonstration. twenty million Americans turn out to hear politicians speak about issues concerning the planet. People participated in everything. From talkathons and prayer vigils to trail hikes. The message was loud and clear. Americans demanded action from their leaders because they were concerned about their environment. As a result, several environmental acts were passed in the 1970s. In 1970 alone Congress responded by establishing the Environmental Protection Agency and passing the Clean Air Act. The Air Pollution Control Act, the Toxic Water Control Act, and an Endangered Species Act followed two decades later.

Earth Day was first celebrated on April 22, 1970. As a result of increased public awareness, the following legislation was passed in the 1970s:
• Clean Air Act
• Water Pollution Control Act
• Toxic Substances Control Act
• Endangered Species Act

Find the 9 errors in this activity. There are no errors in the illustration or the caption.

_____

_____

_____

_____

_____

_____

5. The Burning Phoenix

The phoenix, was a bird in Greek mythology. It was as large or largest than an eagle, and had red and gold feathers. Only one phoenix existed at any time and it was always male. The greek writers said he lived to be four hundred years old. When the life cycle of the phoenix came to a close, he would gather wood and other burnable items and light herself on fire. Out of the ashes, a new phoenix would arise. The new phoenix would then carry the ashes of his father to the sun god. Because of the long life span of the phoenix and his rebirth from the ashes, he symbolized immortality and rebirth. Him was also said to symbolize the raising and setting of the sun.

The Phoenix

The phoenix existed in Greek mythology and was said to live for five hundred years. At the end of the phoenix's life cycle, he would build a fire and burn himself. A new phoenix would arise from the ashes.

Find the 9 errors in this activity. There are no errors in the illustration or the caption.

_____

_____

_____

_____

_____

_____

6. The Missing Cookie Caper

It was a ugly scene. Chocolate fingerprints were smeared on the cookie jar, the kitchen counter, and the younger child's bedroom door. The culprit seems obvious. However, there was a few doubts. Sean, the younger child, was five years old and only forty inches high. The cookie jar was placed on a kitchen shelf. About three feet above the counter. The counter was two feet from the ground. Suspicions began to turn to the older child, Jason. However, Jason was eight years old and only five feet high. Furthermore, Jason's left arm was in a cast. The parent's of the two boys were puzzled. "Who could of done this," they asked?

This drawing shows one possible solution. Here are the clues:

Clue 1: Jason is forty-eight inches high; Sean is forty inches high.

Clue 2: Sean's fingerprints were found on the cookie jar.

Clue 3: Both boys were grinning from ear to ear.

Find the 10 errors in this activity. There are no errors in the illustration or the caption.

_____

_____

_____

_____

_____

_____

7. America's First Colony

Jamestown, founded in 1607 was the first permanent English colony in America. A group of English investors formed the London Company to seek profit in the new land. They sent Capt John Smith and a group of settlers to establish a colony in what is now virginia. The new settlers struggled with hunger, disease, and attacks by the natives. The greater of these threats to the little settlement's survival was disease. Even with the arrival of two additional groups of settlers, the population declined. The settlers were determine, however, to survive. Many was indentured servants for who there was no going back. They had sold their labor, in exchange for free passage to the new land. Five years after the founding, the London Company gave each colonist a parcel of land. Many of the colonists started raising tobacco. This proved to be a very profitable crop, and the colony finally began to thrive.

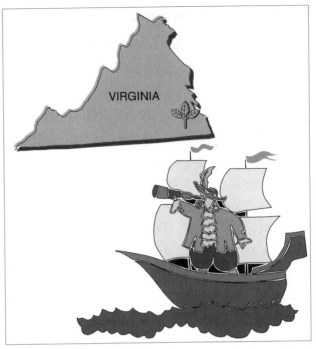

In 1607, Captain John Smith established Jamestown, which became the first lasting English colony in America. In 1611, the settlers were given their own land and started growing tobacco.

Find the 9 errors in this activity. There are no errors in the illustration or the caption.

_____

_____

_____

_____

_____

_____

8. A.S.A.P. for the S.P.C.A.!

What are you do this summer? Does the thought of rescuing wild animals, caring for stray cats and dogs, or helping out with a charitable event sound fun? If you are an animal lover and would like to get involved in one of the best charitable organizations in town, then join the Society for the Prevention of Cruelty to animals with over 200 animals living at our facility, we are always in need of good volunteers. Handling dogs and cats, caring for wildlife, and working with the public is opportunities available to some of our new volunteers. After you see these animals, you will want to become they're friend. In return, they will be good friends to yourself. Our next volunteer orientation is monday, June 2 at 2:00 P.M. in are education building. Playful paws and a good time awaits your arrival!

Hurry along to the S.P.C.A. Volunteer Orientation!

We need you!

WHEN: June 2
WHERE:
Administration building of the S.P.C.A.
TIME: 2:00 P.M.

Training is available to all new volunteers. Choose from any one of the following activities:
- How to handle dogs
- How to care for wildlife
- How to work with the general public

Find the 11 errors in this activity. There are no errors in the illustration or the caption.

_____

_____

_____

_____

_____

_____

9. A Foot in the Door

1555 Revolution Road
San Diego CA 92115
June 11, 1998

Dr. Emelda Walsh
Community Hospital of San Francisco
San Francisco, CA 94150

Dear Dr. Walsh,

As a recent graduate in the field of medicine, I was pleased to see an opening for a Medical Technician at your hospital.

My experience in the field of health begun in 1994 when I were a volunteer for the childrens' cancer ward at Grossmont Hospital. For the last five years I been working as a medical technician for the San Diego Hospital.

I recognize and greatly admire the work that the Community Hospital of San Francisco has been doing since its start in 1908. I look forward to speaking with you regarding my qualifications.

Sincerely
Antonio Brainsworthy

"I've been working on this letter all day," Antonio said with exasperation. "I hope my six years of experience in the field of health will be enough to get my foot in the door."

Find the 10 errors in this activity. There are no errors in the illustration or the caption.

_____

_____

_____

_____

_____

_____

10. How to Catch a Wave

The first steps in learning how to surf is balancing on the surfboard and paddling. To begin, lay horizontally along the center of the board. To balance, place your feet on either side of the board. Paddling done with alternating left and right strokes. After you paddled out, you should face the ocean and start looking for a wave. When you see a good wave turn yourself and your board towards the beach and begin paddling as strong and faster as you can. Arch your back to keep the nose of your board from going underwater, and the wave will give you a nice push and when you feel the force of the wave, you should lift yourself up and place your feet sideways on the board. Keep your board steady. And just ahead of the breaking wave. Your knees should be bent, and your torso should be straight up. Now hang loose, and don't wipe out!

Remember, your feet and legs should be close together while paddling in order to balance the board. While surfing the wave, keep your knees bent and your torso slightly forward.

Find the 10 errors in this activity. There are no errors in the illustration or the caption.

_____

_____

_____

_____

_____

_____

11. The Monarch

In the spring, butterflys seem to be everywhere, but where do they live during the winter? In Autumn, flocks of north american monarch butterflies migrate south to milder climates. One of their destinations are Pacific Grove, California where they will remain until spring. They hibernate in trees in the parks and surrounding areas. In some areas, special butterfly habitats have been set aside to protect these weekly visitors. When you visit these habitats, you see what look like large clusters of dried leafs hanging from the trees. In fact, these clusters are hundreds of butterflies with their wings closed. The dull underpart of the monarch's wing. Resembles a dead leaf and provides the butterfly with protective camouflage while it is rest. The butterflies hang down in overlapping layers from the tree branches. They will hibernate this way until spring arrived. When the butterflies wings are warm by the sun, they will begin to fly again.

Few North American butterflies can live through the cold winter. They usually migrate to warmer climates in the southern United States and Central America. Each year, monarchs and other butterflies spend the winter hibernating in trees, barns, and other dark, sheltered places until spring.

Find the 12 errors in this activity. There are no errors in the illustration or the caption.

_____

_____

_____

_____

_____

_____

12. Drumming It In

Most of my drumming moves was okay, but I wanted to get even better. I was pretty excited when my instructor showed up at 430. "Hey, professor, I'm so glad you came to learn me to play!" I said. He got to the point. "Let's see how you play now, and then we'll improve it," he said. I played Tapper's Suite better than ever, but my skill went unnoticed. "First," he said, "You must set the drum at elbow level. Then we'll worked on your arms and hands." We positioned the drum, and I played again. "Your left hand your weaker is lagging," he said, "and, what's worse, your holding the stick wrong." He made me hold my elbows in grip the sticks securely, and strike with the same force from each hand. I was happier before I knew how worse I was.

Before the teacher corrected him, the student played with elbows too close to the body and with a loose grip, as shown above.

Find the 12 errors in this activity. There are no errors in the illustration or the caption.

_____

_____

_____

_____

_____

_____

13. Spiders and Crabs

Spiders and crabs can look very similar and are, in fact, both classify as arthropods. Arthropods are invertebrate animals that have jointed legs and segmented bodies. Both a spider and a crab has two main body section, the cephalothorax and the abdomen. The cephalothorax is a combined head and chest to which the legs are attach. The spider has ten legs, and the crab has eight. All arthropods also have inner shells called exoskeletons that protect and support its bodies, improve locomotion, and shed periodically as they grow and crabs have compound eyes that consist of many lenses, but spiders eyes have only one lens each. Unlike other types of arthropods, spiders don't have no antennae. However, crabs usually have two pairs of antennae on their heads. The crabs use this antennae as sense organs.

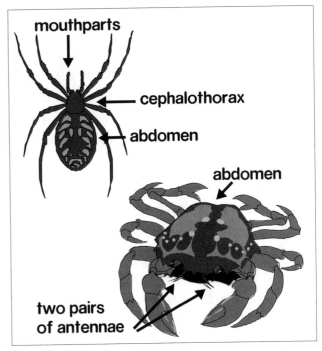

Spiders and crabs are both arthropods and look similar in their general body structure. They both have jointed legs, segmented bodies, and outer shells called exoskeletons.

Find the 11 errors in this activity. There are no errors in the illustration or the caption.

_____

_____

_____

_____

_____

_____

14. The Giant of His Age

Leonardo da Vinci was a painter, a sculptor, a mathematician, a scientist, an engineer, a philosopher, and many other things. He was knowed in popular culture for his paintings including many that are still widely recognized. His most famous painting was the Whistler's Mother. He was known for providing early models of technological advances that included the airplane, the automobile, and the parachute he also proposes using simple machines, such as pulleys and levers, to do complex tasks. One of his ideas were the wheel-driven machine, which would use the turning of a wheel to produce energy. In addition, Leonardo famous for his enormous number of drawings of the human body, including illustrations of the functions of bones and organs. His drawings were considered to be the first accurate portrayals of human anatomy. Because of the many contributions to ours progress, Leonardo was a man to who we owe many thanks.

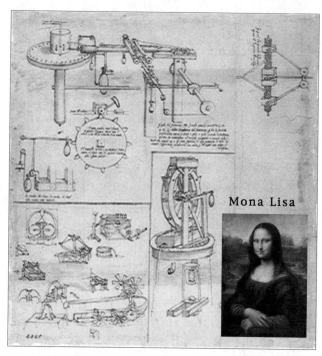

Mona Lisa

Above are shown Leonardo da Vinci's most famous painting and some drawings for a wheel-driven machine. During the Industrial Revolution, factories began using this wheel-driven technology to produce hydroelectric power.

Find the 9 errors in this activity. There are no errors in the illustration or the caption.

15. Night Fright

Deep in the night, she hears the sound of water roaring through the hallway. Saraya peeked out her door. The hallway was as dry as it been since she arrived earlier that day. It was even deeper in the night. When she heard the horrible scream. She called out, and her voice echoed in the silence. It was almost morning when she felt her bed shake. She jumped up, threw open the door, and ran into the hall. Trying to ignore the intensifying screech behind her, she zoomed. Down the long stairway, and into the courtyard. She considered climbing over the wall that surrounded the castle but decided against it. Frantic, she ran along the wall until she stumbled and fell. She heard the noises right behind her and turned around to face hers fate and behind her, her brother was smiling and holding a CD player that was playing "Sounds in the night." "That's not fair Mohammed." Saraya cried. Mohammed just laughed. "We'll leave tomorrow. You'll see," Saraya said, planning to ask mom and dad to cut the visit in half.

On the morning before Saraya's fright, her family arrived at this Scottish castle for a two-week vacation.

Find the 12 errors in this activity. There are no errors in the illustration or the caption.

_____

_____

_____

_____

_____

_____

16. A Net Gain

In a stunning upset in the National Junior Tennis Championships, Marie O'Neal defeated heavy favored Alicia Alfonso. O'Neal upset two other favored players. On the way to her first national crown. In the title match, she lost her serve only in the last game of the second set. Alfonsos serve in contrast was broken once in the first set and once in the third set and she had not lost her serve in the previous three matches. O'Neal was happy that her hard work paid off. "This makes me very proud", she said, and I hope to do as well next year." Alfonso thought his opponent deserved to win and said, "Marie played very well today. She kept the ball deep, and won the big points. She has a tough lefty serve." O'Neal planned to take some time off to enjoy her big win. Alfonso planned to return to her Columbus home to continue training. Both players will try to qualify for the U.S. Open later this year.

Marie O'Neal, 14, of Sarasota, Florida, prepares to serve to defending champion Alicia Alfonso, 17, of Cincinnati, Ohio. They played in the finals of the National Junior Tennis Championships in Providence, R.I. O'Neal upset Alfonso 6-4, 4-6, 7-5.

Find the 11 errors in this activity. There are no errors in the illustration or the caption.

_____

_____

_____

_____

_____

_____

17. A Glimpse into the Past

MACHU PICCHU:
MYSTERY OF THE ANCIENT WORLD

SOUTH AMERICA

Machu Picchu

The Incas built Machu Picchu, in what is now Peru, as a mountain hideaway. It remained undiscovered until 1911. The pictures above are the ones Azzi sent to Linda.

Tucson, Arizona
January 29, 2001

Dear Linda

I haven't written since my letter of December 22, 2000 because I've been busy writing a report about Machu Picchu. This hidden city is 8,000 feet high and was built by the Incas in South Africa. The Incas were conquered in the 1500s, but many of them fled to this secret city. It remained undiscovered for about another 500 years. I read and am sending you "Secrets of the past," an article that gives many facts about the ruins. As you can see, it shows a stone wall with a man who is only half as tall. I also read Inca Treasures, a story about a Inca man. I liked the story but learned more from the article. Both gave me a glimpse of the world of the Incas. Their lives were far different from our in Tucson, Arizona today!

Your Friend,
Azzi

Find the 11 errors in this activity. There are no errors in the illustration or the caption.

_____

_____

_____

_____

_____

_____

18. A Sucker for Squid

A hidden video camera finally captured the thief whod been stealing the octopus food. Over the last few days a lab assistant had noticed something strange. Pieces of squid were missing from the jar of food each morning kept near the octopus tank. He set up a hidden video camera. To monitor the lab one night. The next day, the mystery was solved. The octopus had found a small opening in the cover of its tank. During the night, it would squeeze through the opening. Like all octopuses, it was able to compress all of it's body except the back. Fortunately for the octopus, the opening were large enough for the mouth to fit through. Sliding its tentacles through first, it had pulled the rest of its body through the opening. Using the suckers on its legs, the octopus had then grasped the lid of the jar, pulls it off removed a piece of squid, and proceeded to snack. When it was done eating, the octopus had climbed back inside the tank.

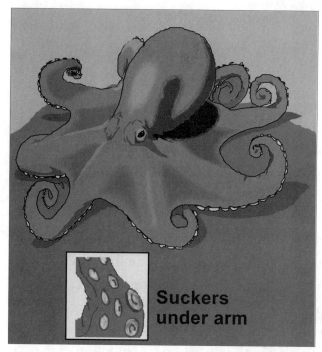

Suckers under arm

Along each of its arms, an octopus has suckers that it uses to grasp things. The only hard part on an octopus's body is its mouth, which is similar to a bird's beak. The rest of the octopus's body is made of soft tissue that can be easily compressed.

Find the 10 errors in this activity. There are no errors in the illustration or the caption.

_____

_____

_____

_____

_____

_____

19. The Eagle Nebula

As I clicked through the television channels, my favorite science show appeared. "The Hubble Space Telescope launched in 1990, has recorded. Many astounding images for we earthbound humans", the announcer was saying. "One such image is this picture of the Eagle Nebula, outside the Milky Way galaxy". A brilliant vision of the nebula filled my screen as he continued. "Radiation from nearby stars cause these enormous towers of gas and dust to glow, notice the globules of gas at the top of the rightmost tower. Each glob may contain new forming stars and are about the size of our solar system!" Wow! Where else could I learn as much as I do from "Outer Visions?"

gaseous globules

Here is the image that appeared on "Outer Visions." These pillars of gas and dust belong to the Eagle Nebula, residing in our Milky Way. They were revealed by the Hubble Space Telescope, placed in orbit in 1990.

Find the 12 errors in this activity. There are no errors in the illustration or the caption.

_____

_____

_____

_____

_____

_____

20. Deadly Dino

Tyrannosaurus rex was the most feared predator of it's time. It could run very fast on its powerful hind legs and its sharp teeth were effective in catching its food and *Tyrannosaurus rex* and other dinosaurs first appeared about 200 million years ago. They became extinct. About 65 million years ago. For more than 135 million years, dinosaurs ruled the world. *Tyrannosaurus rex* was the King of them all. The T-rex, as it are popularly called, had two long hind legs that it used for walking or running and two longer front legs that it used for attacking its prey. Even at 20 feet tall the T-rex was not the taller of all dinosaurs. That was a honor belonging to *Brachiosaurus*, which could have looked over a building three stories high. The ability to reach tall plants for food made T-rex the most feared predator of prehistoric times.

A painting of *Tyrannosaurus rex*, often called T-rex, is shown above. T-rex was a carnivore and fed on other dinosaurs.

Find the 11 errors in this activity. There are no errors in the illustration or the caption.

_____

_____

_____

_____

_____

_____

21. Victory on Wheels

Amy was fast that day. In fact, she had never rode faster. "she rides like the wind" her husband said as she whizzed by. She had been trailing the pack by more than 30 seconds. She thrust her fists in the air and yelled excitedly as she came across the finish line twenty:six seconds before the next finisher. It was her second victory in a bicycle race. She and her husband tried to decide what contributed to her great finish. "Was it what I ate"? she asked. "Maybe it was because you were well rested, he said. They decided that her success was probably a combination of all the possibilities and that made it difficult to duplicate. Anyway, victory is her. Amy's mind was already racing to the womens' triathlon that would take place in three weeks. Would she make it her next victory?

Amy was in the lead for the entire 20-mile competition. She cruised to a first-place finish in 48 minutes, 45 seconds. She was just catching her breath when the next finisher came in at 49 minutes, 7 seconds.

Find the 12 errors in this activity. There are no errors in the illustration or the caption.

_____

_____

_____

_____

_____

_____

22. An Archaeological Find

Today, our exacting field work in Australia was reward. We spent most of the day carefully uncovering what seemed to be an ancient knife. We had many questions. When was it made? Was it used as a weapon? Was it used for cooking? Once the knife uncovered, we noticed another object just below it. It was a small wood carving in the shape of a dingo, a dog brought to Australia by the Aborigines about 5000 to 8000 years ago. We theorized that the knife was most likely used to carve the wooden dog. However we had no indication of the carvings age. We will had to use the tree ring dating method to find out how old the carving actually is. Every wooden object has tree rings. Each ring represents one year of growth. We will compare the rings of the carving to the rings of a faraway tree to see were they match and we are eager to find out how old this artifacts really are. What more will we discover?

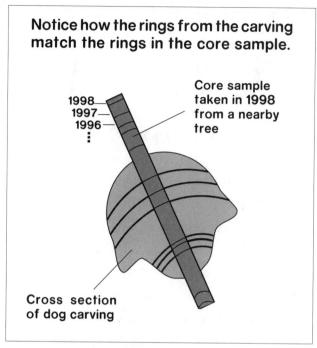

Notice how the rings from the carving match the rings in the core sample.

1998
1997
1996

Core sample taken in 1998 from a nearby tree

Cross section of dog carving

The core sample is laid on a cross section of the carving to see where the rings match. Since the age of the core sample is known, the scientists can count backward the number of rings (years) to see how old the artifact is. The carving turns out to be quite new!

Find the 10 errors in this activity. There are no errors in the illustration or the caption.

_____

_____

_____

_____

_____

_____

23. An Early American

We could hardly wait to hear the author of "Early Americanimals!" "Had you lived during the 1830s you might have seen great herds of bison grazing between the Appalachian Mountains and the Rockies," he began. "Though many of these majestic creatures were wiped out, some is around today." We interrupted him. "How would you know a pair of bison if themselves walked down your street?" we asked. "Well," he answered, "Most bisons' hair is coarse and brown. Each have a hump on the back. Three horns adorn each massive head, and the bison wear beards under their chins. A bull weighs close to a ton, but a cow weighs twice as much. When provoked, each of the two bisons could probably run quite fastly. Let's hope that you would run the faster"! We were glad that our hero had both knowledge and a sense of humor.

According to "Early Americanimals," what we call the American buffalo is more correctly identified as the bison. The males are bulls, and the females are cows. Males often weigh nearly 2000 pounds, and females weigh about 1000 pounds. Bison have dark brown coats and rough hair.

Find the 13 errors in this activity. There are no errors in the illustration or the caption.

_____

_____

_____

_____

_____

_____

24. A Profitable Platform

Dear Editor:

As part of my campaign platform for student body president, I would like to propose that students be paid for attending school. My mom is always telling me that school is my job. Students would learn much fast than usual if they got paid for it, and they would get valuable experience in earning a living. If I had been pay $5.00 for each hour I attended school last semester, I would have earned a whole lot more than I did. Instead my parents paid me only $11.00 for the two A's that I got on my report card last semester. The thing is is the school could establish a salary scale that was base on letter grades and pay each of us students an hourly wage based on their previous semester's academic performance. My would sure improve. I hope the school administration will give my request due consideration and that the students be able to vote on this important issue.

Justin is already imagining how much money he will have for his college fund if the school votes in favor of salaries for students. "I'll earn a lot more on an hourly basis than the $5.00 for each of the two A's that I got last semester."

Sincerely:
Justin Case

Find the 11 errors in this activity. There are no errors in the illustration or the caption.

25. Heart-Racing Journey

With the goal of studying a microscopic society, I prepare for transport. I am successfully shrinked, but something gone wrong with the coordinates! I materialize in the right atrium of a chambered muscular organ. What could of happened? Suddenly, all is still, and I brace for a contraction. The jolt hurls the blood cells and I past the mitral valve into the right ventricle. Hey I have somehow survived! The ventricle squeezes the blood and myself toward the lungs, were I can be saved. Our engineer will surely locate and beam me out once I'm there. I am propelled with a rush but slow down just at the pulmonary valve. Its two cusps trap myself like doors as me struggle to get out! I am not to be defeated, though. With a mighty effort, I pull my hips through and then my legs, to. I am free of the heart! I glide to the lungs, sure that I will soon be saved.

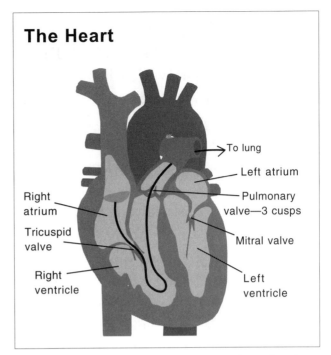

The Heart

The black arrow shows the path of the hapless investigator, who was finally identified in a lung, relocated to the transport room of the mother ship, and maximized in size.

Find the 12 errors in this activity. There are no errors in the illustration or the caption.

26. Schedule It!

Did she like being disorganized? Did she enjoy doing homework when her friends said, "Let's go dancing?" No, she did not. On the other hand, she felt overwhelmed with things to do. Her father, whom was a good advisor, came to the rescue with an article called Doing It All". He said, "Prioritize your activities, and then leave go of the things that matter the less. Schedule the important things first, and fit the other stuff around them." Soon, Juanita was penning activities on her schedule. She managed to include at least one fun thing each day. On Thursdays, she would surf at 330 and watch her favorite television show right after dinner. Instead of arguing and playing with her brother after doing dishes, she would practice her music for an hour. She was pleased as she closed her eyes that night. "Tomorrow," Juanita said to himself, "Things would be different."

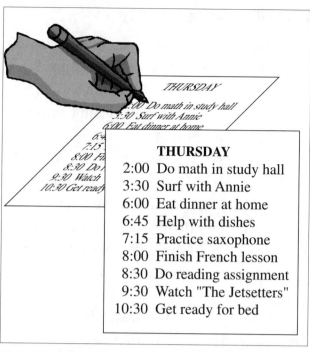

THURSDAY	
2:00	Do math in study hall
3:30	Surf with Annie
6:00	Eat dinner at home
6:45	Help with dishes
7:15	Practice saxophone
8:00	Finish French lesson
8:30	Do reading assignment
9:30	Watch "The Jetsetters"
10:30	Get ready for bed

The above illustration shows both Juanita's penciled version and her final printout of the schedule for Thursdays.

Find the 13 errors in this activity. There are no errors in the illustration or the caption.

_____

_____

_____

_____

_____

_____

27. Bales of Fun

Rural Route 1
Canton, NY, 13617
June 11, 1998

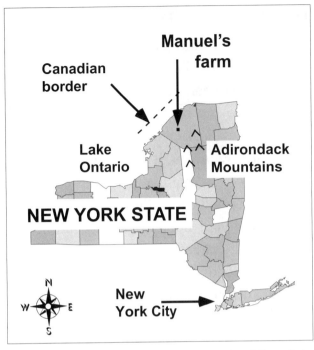

Manuel's farm is in the largest county of the state of New York.

Dear Pham

    I'll bet your city is very exciting, but, believe me living in rural St Lawrence County can be great. We are located northwest of Lake Ontario between the Adirondack Mts and New York City. I and my sister work here on our dairy farm every day. At milking time, I spread the straw while Cindy carries pails of milk. When we do the haying, Cindy picks up bales weighing a hundred pounds each and hoists them onto the wagon. I drive the tractor pulling the wagon drinking iced tea. At the barn, I watch the bales raise to the loft on the hay elevator. I leave Cindy have the honor of catching and neatly stacking the bales in the 100° heat of the barn. It's a great life for him and I! I don't understand why Cindy can't wait to go to college in the city.

                Sincerely,
                Manuel

Find the 13 errors in this activity. There are no errors in the illustration or the caption.

_____

_____

_____

_____

_____

_____

28. A Lesson on Haiku

"Is this a haiku poem" Mr. Zaluski asked the class. The student's eyes scanned the poem in their literature books. "how is a haiku poem arranged?" the teacher questions. "A haiku poem has seventeen syllables. It's arranged in three line of five, six, and five syllables each" Roberto replied. "Excellent Roberto. You been doing your homework. The haiku is a traditional form of japanese poetry that was developed in the 1700s by a man named Basho. What do you notice about haiku"? Mr. Zaluski asked. "It's simple," Shakira stated. "Yes, the haiku seems simple because there are few words. However, it is meant to express something much more". Carmen rose to the challenge. "Maybe the poet is try to express serenity. On the other hand, maybe the flower is meant to symbolize renewal of life." Mr. Zaluski smiled. His class was really catching on.

Rising from the pond...
A flower spreads its petals
Taking in the sun.

–Anonymous

The poetry known as haiku was developed in the 17th century. Haiku is unrhymed and is typically based on nature or the seasons.

Find the 14 errors in this activity. There are no errors in the illustration or the caption.

_____

_____

_____

_____

_____

_____

29. Eclipsed!

Stargazers from all over the world converged near Hilo, Hawaii during the full Moon to view a partial solar eclipse. They came to spend a chilly morning in the observatory atop the volcano Mauna Kea, which is nearly 14,000 feet tall. As the Sun hid more and more of the Moon, the cheers began. When the eclipse were total, the cheers became an deafening roar. It was a rare totally eclipse visible from the Northern and Western Hemispheres. Most eclipses can usually be seen only in the Southern Hemisphere. The location was a real plus for Gin-Wei Chang, a devoted Observer. "I've seen five in a row now, and this one is the better because I didn't have to travel so far", she said. "Last time, I had to watch from an island in the indian Ocean." For all their preparation and excitement, the observers had little time to enjoy the view. The Sun's total disappearance, which began at 1107 A.M., lasted only 4 minutes.

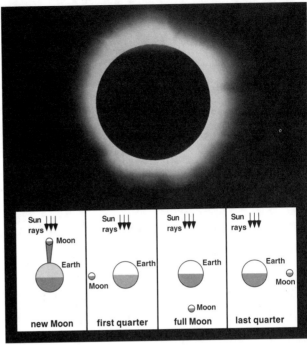

At top is a photo of the solar event that took place near Hilo, Hawaii. The diagram shows the four main Moon phases, which occur every month. During a total solar eclipse, the Moon, Earth, and Sun are perfectly aligned. As a result, the Moon blocks out any view of the Sun. Thus, the total solar eclipse is possible during only one of these Moon phases.

Find the 12 errors in this activity. There are no errors in the illustration or the caption.

_____

_____

_____

_____

_____

_____

30. Footnotes in Anatomy

"Next we're going to discuss the human foot, which has 24 bones in all," said Mrs. Langdon. "They can be divided into three different kinds." As she pointed at the ankle Mrs. Langdon said, "Can anyone give the name for the ankle bones" Becky answered that they were the tarsals. "That's right," Mrs. Langdon said. "The foot has seven tarsal bones. What about the instep bones? Miguel correctly identified them as the metatarsals. "That's right again," Mrs. Langdon said. "The foot has five metatarsal bones. Whom knows what we call the bones in our toes?" Nobody knew, so Mrs. Langdon continued. "The toe bones are called phalanges. The foot have fourteen phalanges. To are in the big toe, and three are in each of the other four toes. Can anyone guess why the big toe had one fewest bone than the rest of the toes? Oh, there's the bell. Well have to take up that subject on Monday. "Have a great weekend"!

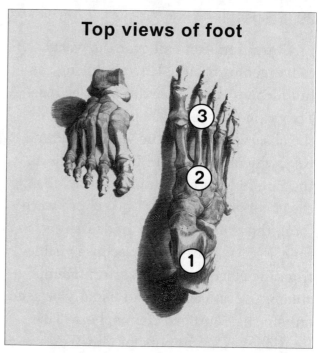

Top views of foot

The human foot has 26 bones, which can be divided into three categories: (1) tarsals, (2) metatarsals, and (3) phalanges, pronounced FUH-LAN-JEES.

Find the 13 errors in this activity. There are no errors in the illustration or the caption.

_____

_____

_____

_____

_____

_____

31. Digits Rule in CD

I thought that all I needed was my music but professor Alverson changed my mind. He got my friends and I interested in science. He explained the digital audio technology used in recording and playing back sounds. "A compact disc contains many tiny pits and raised areas "called lands" he said. "It is read by a system that shines a laser beam on the pits and lands as the disc spins by. When the laser beam encounters a pit or a land," he continued, its reflection is changed. The system interprets the change as a 1 or a 0. The CD player uses the information not only to interpret the message, but also to reconstruct it." I'm glad my CD player may translate the analog language into the digital music I and my friends love to hear!

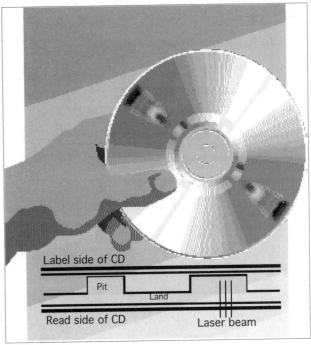

A compact disc is made of aluminum that is coated with acrylic. A laser mechanism reads the disc by shining its beam through the coating and onto the track of pits and lands. A CD player translates the digital message into the analog sounds we hear.

Find the 11 errors in this activity. There are no errors in the illustration or the caption.

_____

_____

_____

_____

_____

_____

32. Count on Computers

We humans like to make things easy for us. Because we have eight fingers and two thumbs, we use the decimal number system. It is based on ten digits. Computers, however, are more suited to the binary, or base two, system. Base two requires only one symbol. A one or a zero can easily in the computer be expressed as either a flow of electricity and no flow of electricity. How do we read an number in base two? On the most far right is the ones place. The next place to the left are the twos place. The third place shows how many fours, the fourth place shows how many eights, and so on. We add all the values that hold ones to get the equivalent decimal number. Therefore, the binary number in the illustration represents our decimal number twenty-two. Since only two states of electric flow need to be used, The binary number system lets computers process information most easiest than they could otherwise. Computers, in turn, can make things easier for ourselves. Awesome

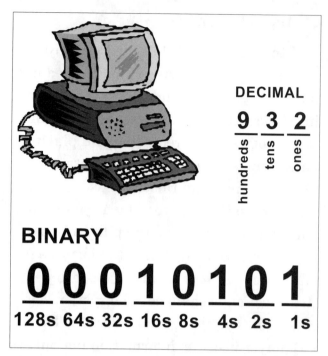

DECIMAL

9 3 2

hundreds | tens | ones

BINARY

0 0 0 1 0 1 0 1

128s 64s 32s 16s 8s 4s 2s 1s

Two different numbers are shown, a decimal number on the upper right and a binary number below. The binary number system uses the symbols 1 and 0. For each 1, add the decimal value of its place (shown below the blank). This binary number represents the sum of 1, 4, and 16.

Find the 12 errors in this activity. There are no errors in the illustration or the caption.

_____

_____

_____

_____

_____

_____

33. Animated about Art

We were excited to hear about jobs at Magic Carpet Studios! We readily lended our ears to supervisor Warren of the animation team. "Layout artists make sketches of all scenes for the animated film. Background artists create tone and style and the animators design the characters. Have you any idea how much research is necessary for the animator's job"? he asked. We told him "that we already knowed of artists whom practically lived with deers to learn their movements. "The animators draw the extreme movements," he continued, but the background artists make all the intermediate drawings. Finally, it is the cleanup artist who draws the more careful of all. This artist must redraw the art and add the final touches. For example," he said as he pointed at a pig's suspenders, "these three buttons must be added at cleanup. It is the cleanup artist who's work will be saw by yourselves, the audience."

The animation supervisor described various artists' tasks, as listed below. The scene above was used to illustrate the cleanup artist's job.
- layout artist: sketch of scenes
- background artist: overall tone & style
- animator: characters, extreme movements
- inbetweener: intermediate movements
- cleanup artist: painstaking detail work

Find the 15 errors in this activity. There are no errors in the illustration or the caption.

_____

_____

_____

_____

_____

_____

ANSWERS

This answer key provides the following information for each activity: the number and types of errors, a paragraph using superscribed numbers to show the locations of the errors, a number key explaining each error, a bracketed reference to the corresponding section of the Grammar Guide, and the corrected paragraph.

Note that in the error count below, a run-on sentence or a sentence fragment is counted as one error even though the correction may require two changes, e.g., adding or deleting a period and a capital letter.

The errors in English mechanics in *Editor in Chief® B2* have been geared to correspond to an intermediate-level English curriculum. For further information about the rules of grammar, usage, and punctuation covered in this book, see the Grammar Guide pp. 61–84.

1. Do Elephants Mourn?

9 errors—1 content; 2 grammar; 1 punctuation; 3 spelling; 2 usage

Do Elephants Mourn? Errors

Do elephants mourn the loss of other elephants? Its[1] a question that has no definite answer, but fascinating behaviors have been observe[2]. Their[3] is[4] documented cases of elephants gathering around the body of a deceased elephant and staying with it for as long as a weak[5] to protect it from scavengers. Seeing the remains of a tusk has prompted some elephants to stop, pick the tusk up with their trunks, caress them[6], and then pass it among themselves. Some elephants have been observed.[7] Trying to pick up a fallen and wounded elephant with their tails[8] in an attempt to get the fallen elephant to its feet again. Perhaps we will never know if elephants mourn, but it is an interesting question to ponder. What do yourselves[9] think?

1. *It's*—Spelling [6.1]
2. been *observed*—Grammar: past participle (in present perfect passive voice) [3.22, 3.24, 3.25]
3. *There*—Spelling [6.1]
4. *are*—Usage: agreement of verb with subject in number (cases/are) [4.2]
5. *week*—Spelling [6.1]
6. *it*—Usage: agreement of pronoun with noun in number [4.1]
7. *observed trying*—Punctuation: sentence fragment [5.38]
8. *trunks*—Content: see caption [2.1]
9. *you*—Grammar: pronoun as subject (not reflexive) [3.19, 3.20]

Do Elephants Mourn? Corrected

Do elephants mourn the loss of other elephants? It's a question that has no definite answer, but fascinating behaviors have been observed. There are documented cases of elephants gathering around the body of a deceased elephant and staying with it for as long as a week to protect it from scavengers. Seeing the remains of a tusk has prompted some elephants to stop, pick the tusk up with their trunks, caress it, and then pass it among themselves. Some elephants have been observed trying to pick up a fallen and wounded elephant with their trunks in an attempt to get the fallen elephant to its feet again. Perhaps we will never know if elephants mourn, but it is an interesting question to ponder. What do you think?

2. Up in Arms

10 errors—2 content; 3 grammar; 2 punctuation; 3 usage

Up in Arms Errors

31 Post Road
Cambridge, MA 02138
August 4, 1999

Dear Kaneesha,

I was very happy to get the new job, but I have felt like an octopus this[1] last three weeks. It started out easy enough, but then Ms. Atkins piled the work higher and higher. The sketch shows. [2]Me dealing with the usual five[3] phones at a time! I wouldn't mind so much if the boss did some of the work himself[4]. However, she often puts her feet up or even lays[5] down for a nap. She says to me, "Why, you do almost as better[6] a job as I do!" Isn't that awful[7] insulting? Working here is neither fun or[8] profitable, and I could[9] care less for the job. It's time to look for a new one.

Your friend[10]
Johann

1. *these*—Usage: agreement of demonstrative adjective with noun (*these/weeks*) **[4.5]**
2. *shows me*—Punctuation: sentence fragment **[5.38]**
3. *four*—Content: see illustration **[2.1]**
4. *herself*—Usage: agreement of reflexive pronoun with antecedent (*she/herself*) **[4.1]**
5. *lies*—Usage: confused word pairs (*lays/lies*) **[4.8]**
6. *good*—Grammar: positive adjective (not comparative) **[3.1, 3.8, 3.9]**
7. *awfully*—Grammar: adverb modifies adjective **[3.4]**
8. *nor*—Grammar: correlative conjunctions used in pairs (*neither/nor*) **[3.11]**
9. *couldn't*—Content: see caption (if he cares not at all then he could *not* care less) **[2.1]**
10. *friend,*—Punctuation: comma in closing of friendly letter **[5.12]**

Up in Arms Corrected

31 Post Road
Cambridge, MA 02138
August 4, 1999

Dear Kaneesha,

I was very happy to get the new job, but I have felt like an octopus these last three weeks. It started out easy enough, but then Ms. Atkins piled the work higher and higher. The sketch shows me dealing with the usual four phones at a time! I wouldn't mind so much if the boss did some of the work herself. However, she often puts her feet up or even lies down for a nap. She says to me, "Why, you do almost as good a job as I do!" Isn't that awfully insulting? Working here is neither fun nor profitable, and I couldn't care less for the job. It's time to look for a new one.

Your friend,
Johann

3. Fishy Story

12 errors—2 content; 2 capitalization; 6 grammar; 2 puctuation;

Fishy Story Errors

I had been diving in the [1]south pacific[1] and studying the local sea life. I'm afraid I come[2] a bit closer to a certain form of sea life than I truly desired. Lets[3] call her Wanda. Though I moved the fast[4] I have ever moved, I could not escape the gaping jaws. Thirtyfour[5] teeth then surrounded me, and them[6] threatened to clamp down harder at any moment. My snorkeling[7] gear seemed to be squeezing my head most[8] tightly than ever. Mine[9] arms were just about to give out. Fortunately, captain[10] Gormand[11] appeared and came quick[12] to my rescue. He was able to prop Wanda's mouth open with a long beam while I escaped. Wanda is probably now telling her friends about the one that got away!

1. *South Pacific*—Capital: proper noun **[1.3]**
2. *came*—Grammar: past tense verb **[3.24]**
3. *Let's*—Punctuation: apostrophe in contraction **[5.1]**
4. *fastest*—Grammar: superlative adverb **[3.9, 3.4]**
5. *Thirty-four*—Punctuation: hyphen used in compound number **[5.25]**
6. *they*—Grammar: pronoun as subject **[3.19]**
7. *scuba*—Content: see illustration **[2.1]**
8. *more*—Grammar: comparative adverb **[3.9]**
9. *my*—Grammar: possessive pronoun with noun **[3.19]**
10. *Captain*—Capital: title used as part of a name **[1.6]**
11. *Drake*—Content: see caption **[2.1]**
12. *quickly*—Grammar: adverb modifies verb **[3.4]**

Fishy Story Corrected

I had been diving in the South Pacific and studying the local sea life. I'm afraid I came a bit closer to a certain form of sea life than I truly desired. Let's call her Wanda. Though I moved the fastest I have ever moved, I could not escape the gaping jaws. Thirty-four teeth then surrounded me, and they threatened to clamp down harder at any moment. My scuba gear seemed to be squeezing my head more tightly than ever. My arms were just about to give out. Fortunately, Captain Drake appeared and came quickly to my rescue. He was able to prop Wanda's mouth open with a long beam while I escaped. Wanda is probably now telling her friends about the one that got away!

4. Earth Day Celebration

9 errors—3 content; 2 capitalization; 1 grammar; 3 punctuation

Earth Day Celebration Errors

Earth Day was first celebrated on april[1] 22, 1970[2] as a nationwide street demonstration. twenty[3] million Americans turn[4] out to hear politicians speak about issues concerning the planet. People participated in everything.[5] From talkathons and prayer vigils to trail hikes. The message was loud and clear. Americans demanded action from their leaders because they were concerned about their environment. As a result, several environmental acts were passed in the 1970s. In 1970 alone[6] Congress responded by establishing the Environmental Protection Agency and passing the Clean Air Act. The Air[7] Pollution Control Act, the Toxic Water[8] Control Act, and an Endangered Species Act followed [9]two decades later[9].

1. *April*—Capital: month **[1.8]**
2. *1970,*—Punctuation: comma after year (*month day, year*) in sentence **[5.10]**
3. *Twenty*—Capital: first word of sentence **[1.1]**
4. *turned*—Grammar: past tense verb **[3.24]**
5. *everything from*—Punctuation: sentence fragment **[5.38]**
6. *alone,*—Punctuation: comma used after introductory phrase **[5.15]**
7. *Water*—Content: see caption **[2.1]**
8. *Substances*—Content: see caption **[2.1]**
9. *shortly after.*—Content: see caption (Acceptable: *that same decade, during the 70s,* etc.) **[2.1]**

Earth Day Celebration Corrected

Earth Day was first celebrated on April 22, 1970, as a nationwide street demonstration. Twenty million Americans turned out to hear politicians speak about issues concerning the planet. People participated in everything from talkathons and prayer vigils to trail hikes. The message was loud and clear. Americans demanded action from their leaders because they were concerned about their environment. As a result, several environmental acts were passed in the 1970s. In 1970 alone, Congress responded by establishing the Environmental Protection Agency and passing the Clean Air Act. The Water Pollution Control Act, the Toxic Substances Control Act, and an Endangered Species Act followed shortly after.

5. The Burning Phoenix

9 errors—1 content; 1 capitalization; 2 grammar; 3 punctuation; 2 usage

The Burning Phoenix Errors

The phoenix,[1] was a bird in Greek mythology. It was as large or largest[2] than an eagle,[3] and had red and gold feathers. Only one phoenix existed at any time[4] and it was always male. The greek[5] writers said he lived to be four[6] hundred years old. When the life cycle of the phoenix came to a close, he would gather wood and other burnable items and light herself[7] on fire. Out of the ashes, a new phoenix would arise. The new phoenix would then carry the ashes of his father to the sun god. Because of the long life span of the phoenix and his rebirth from the ashes, he symbolized immortality and rebirth. Him[8] was also said to symbolize the raising[9] and setting of the sun.

1. *phoenix was*—Punctuation: unnecessary comma [5.21]
2. *larger*—Grammar: comparative adjective [3.9]
3. *eagle and*—Punctuation: unnecessary comma [5.21]
4. *time, and*—Punctuation: comma used before coordinating conjunctions joining independent clauses [5.18, 5.33]
5. *Greek*—Capital: proper adjective [1.4]
6. *five*—Content: see caption [2.1]
7. *himself*—Usage: agreement of reflexive pronoun with antecedent [4.1, 3.20]

8. *He*—Grammar: pronoun as subject [3.19]
9. *rising*—Usage: confused word pair (rise/raise) [4.8]

The Burning Phoenix Corrected

The phoenix was a bird in Greek mythology. It was as large or larger than an eagle and had red and gold feathers. Only one phoenix existed at any time, and it was always male. The Greek writers said he lived to be five hundred years old. When the life cycle of the phoenix came to a close, he would gather wood and other burnable items and light himself on fire. Out of the ashes, a new phoenix would arise. The new phoenix would then carry the ashes of his father to the sun god. Because of the long life span of the phoenix and his rebirth from the ashes, he symbolized immortality and rebirth. He was also said to symbolize the rising and setting of the sun.

6. The Missing Cookie Caper

10 errors—2 content; 2 grammar; 4 punctuation; 1 spelling; 1 usage

The Missing Cookie Caper Errors

It was a[1] ugly scene. Chocolate fingerprints were smeared on the cookie jar, the kitchen counter, and the younger child's bedroom door. The culprit seems[2] obvious. However, there was[3] a few doubts. Sean, the younger child, was five years old and only forty inches high. The cookie jar was placed on a kitchen shelf.[4] About three feet above the counter. The counter was two feet from the ground. Suspicions began to turn to the older child, Jason. However, Jason was eight years old and only five[5] feet high. Furthermore, Jason's left[6] arm was in a cast. The parent's[7] of the two boys were puzzled. "Who could of[8] done this,[9]" they asked?[10]

1. *an*—Grammar: article *an* before vowel sound [3.5]

2. *seemed*—Grammar: past tense verb **[3.24]**

3. *were*—Usage: agreement of verb with subject in number **[4.2]**

4. *shelf about*—Punctuation: sentence fragment **[5.38]**

5. *four*—Content: see caption **[2.1]**

6. *right*—Content: see illustration **[2.1]**

7. *parents*—Punctuation: unnecessary apostrophe **[5.3]**

8. could *have*—Spelling/usage **[6.5]**

9. *this?"*—Punctuation: question mark with quoted direct question **[5.29, 5.30]**

10. *asked.*—Punctuation: period ending declarative sentence **[5.26]**

The Missing Cookie Caper Corrected

It was an ugly scene. Chocolate fingerprints were smeared on the cookie jar, the kitchen counter, and the younger child's bedroom door. The culprit seemed obvious. However, there were a few doubts. Sean, the younger child, was five years old and only forty inches high. The cookie jar was placed on a kitchen shelf about three feet above the counter. The counter was two feet from the ground. Suspicions began to turn to the older child, Jason. However, Jason was eight years old and only four feet high. Furthermore, Jason's right arm was in a cast. The parents of the two boys were puzzled. "Who could have done this?" they asked.

7. America's First Colony

9 errors—1 content; 1 capitalization; 3 grammar; 3 punctuation; 1 usage

America's First Colony Errors

Jamestown, founded in 1607[1] was the first permanent English colony in America. A group of English investors formed the London Company to seek profit in the new land. They sent Capt[2] John Smith and a group of settlers to establish a colony in what is now [3]virginia. The new settlers struggled with

hunger, disease, and attacks by the natives. The greater[4] of these threats to the little settlement's survival was disease. Even with the arrival of two additional groups of settlers, the population declined. The settlers were determine[5], however, to survive. Many was[6] indentured servants for who[7] there was no going back. They had sold their labor,[8] in exchange for free passage to the new land. Five[9] years after the founding, the London Company gave each colonist a parcel of land. Many of the colonists started raising tobacco. This proved to be a very profitable crop, and the colony finally began to thrive.

1. *1607,*—Punctuation: comma with nonessential appositive **[5.16]**

2. *Capt.*—Punctuation: period after abbreviation (Acceptable: *Captain*) **[5.27]**

3. *Virginia*—Capital: proper noun **[1.3]**

4. *greatest* of these—Grammar: superlative adjective **[3.9]**

5. were *determined*—Grammar: past participle (in past tense passive voice) **[3.22, 3.24, 3.25]**

6. Many *were*—Usage: agreement of verb with indefinite pronoun **[4.4]**

7. for *whom*—Grammar: pronoun *whom* used as object **[3.21]**

8. *labor in*—Punctuation: unnecessary comma **[5.21]**

9. *Four* years—Content: see caption **[2.1]**

America's First Colony Corrected

Jamestown, founded in 1607, was the first permanent English colony in America. A group of English investors formed the London Company to seek profit in the new land. They sent Capt. John Smith and a group of settlers to establish a colony in what is now Virginia. The new settlers struggled with hunger, disease, and attacks by the natives. The greatest of these threats to the little settlement's survival was disease. Even with the arrival of two additional groups of settlers, the population declined. The settlers were determined, however, to survive. Many were indentured servants for whom there was no going back. They had sold their labor in exchange for free passage to the new land. Four years after the founding, the London Company gave each colonist a parcel of land. Many of the colonists started raising tobacco. This proved to be a very profitable crop, and the colony finally began to thrive.

8. A.S.A.P. for the S.P.C.A.!

11 errors—2 content; 2 capitalization; 2 grammar; 1 punctuation; 2 spelling; 2 usage

A.S.A.P. for the S.P.C.A.! Errors

What are you do[1] this summer? Does the thought of rescuing wild animals, caring for stray cats and dogs, or helping out with a charitable event sound fun? If you are an animal lover and would like to get involved in one of the best charitable organizations in town, then join the Society for the Prevention of Cruelty to animals[2] [3]with over 200 animals living at our facility, we are always in need of good volunteers. Handling dogs and cats, caring for wildlife, and working with the public is[4] opportunities available to some[5] of our new volunteers. After you see these animals, you will want to become they're[6] friend. In return, they will be good friends to yourself[7]. Our next volunteer orientation is [8]monday, June 2 at 2:00 P.M. in are[9] education[10] building. Playful paws and a good time awaits[11] your arrival!

1. *doing*—Grammar: present participle verb (in present progressive tense) (Acceptable: What *will* you do...) **[3.22, 3.24, 3.25]**
2. *Animals*—Capital: proper noun (also see abbreviation S.P.C.A. in illustration) **[1.3]**
3. *Animals. With*—Punctuation: run-on sentence **[5.37]**
4. *are*—Usage: agreement of verb with compound subject **[4.3]**

5. *all*—Content: see caption **[2.1]**
6. *their*—Spelling **[6.1]**
7. *you*—Grammar: pronoun as object (not reflexive) **[3.19, 3.20]**
8. *Monday*—Capital: weekday **[1.8]**
9. *our*—Spelling **[6.1]**
10. *administration*—Content: see caption **[2.1]**
11. *await*—Usage: agreement of verb with compound subject **[4.3]**

A.S.A.P. for the S.P.C.A.! Corrected

What are you doing this summer? Does the thought of rescuing wild animals, caring for stray cats and dogs, or helping out with a charitable event sound fun? If you are an animal lover and would like to get involved in one of the best charitable organizations in town, then join the Society for the Prevention of Cruelty to Animals. With over 200 animals living at our facility, we are always in need of good volunteers. Handling dogs and cats, caring for wildlife, and working with the public are opportunities available to all of our new volunteers. After you see these animals, you will want to become their friend. In return, they will be good friends to you. Our next volunteer orientation is Monday, June 2 at 2:00 P.M. in our administration building. Playful paws and a good time await your arrival!

9. A Foot in the Door

10 errors—1 content; 1 capitalization; 2 grammar; 5 punctuation; 1 usage

A Foot in the Door Errors

1555 Revolution Road
San Diego[1] CA 92115
June 11, 1998

Dr. Emelda Walsh
Community Hospital of San Francisco
San Francisco, CA 94150

Dear Dr. Walsh,[2]
    As a recent graduate in the field of medicine, I was pleased to see an opening

for a [3]Medical Technician[3] at your hospital.

My experience in the field of health begun[4] in 1994[5] when I were[6] a volunteer for the childrens'[7] cancer ward at Grossmont Hospital. For the last five years[8] I [9]been working as a medical technician for the San Diego Hospital.

I recognize and greatly admire the work that the Community Hospital of San Francisco has been doing since its start in 1908. I look forward to speaking with you regarding my qualifications.

Sincerely[10]
Antonio Brainsworthy

1. *San Diego, CA*—Punctuation: comma between elements of address **[5.7]**
2. *Walsh:*—Punctuation: colon in greeting of business letter **[5.5]**
3. *medical technician*—Capital: unnecessary **[1.6]**
4. *began*—Grammar: irregular past tense verb (not past participle) **[3.24]**
5. *1992*—Content: see caption **[2.1]**
6. *was*—Usage: agreement of verb with subject (in adverb clause) **[4.2]**
7. *children's*—Punctuation: apostrophe with possessive of plural not ending in *s* **[5.3]**
8. *years,*—Punctuation: comma used after introductory phrase **[5.15]**
9. *have* been—Grammar: helping verb (in present perfect tense) **[3.26, 3.24]**
10. *Sincerely,*—Punctuation: comma after closing of letter **[5.12]**

A Foot in the Door Corrected

1555 Revolution Road
San Diego, CA 92115
June 11, 1998

Dr. Emelda Walsh
Community Hospital of San Francisco
San Francisco, CA 94150

Dear Dr. Walsh:

As a recent graduate in the field of medicine, I was pleased to see an opening for a medical technician at your hospital.

My experience in the field of health began in 1992 when I was a volunteer for the children's cancer ward at Grossmont Hospital. For the last five years, I have been working as a medical technician for the San Diego Hospital.

I recognize and greatly admire the work that the Community Hospital of San Francisco has been doing since its start in 1908. I look forward to speaking with you regarding my qualifications.

Sincerely,
Antonio Brainsworthy

10. How to Catch a Wave

10 errors—2 content; 3 grammar; 3 punctuation; 2 usage

How to Catch a Wave Errors

The first steps in learning how to surf is[1] balancing on the surfboard and paddling. To begin, lay[2] horizontally along the center of the board. To balance, place your feet [3]on either side of[3] the board. Paddling [4]done with alternating left and right strokes. After you [5]paddled out, you should face the ocean and start looking for a wave. When you see a good wave[6] turn yourself and your board towards the beach and begin paddling as strong and faster[7] as you can. Arch your back to keep the nose of your board from going underwater, and the wave will give you a nice push[8] and when you feel the force of the wave, you should lift yourself up and place your feet sideways on the board. Keep your board steady. [9]And just ahead of the breaking wave. Your knees should be bent, and your torso should be straight up[10]. Now hang loose, and don't wipe out!

1. *are*—Usage: agreement of verb with subject in number **[4.2]**
2. *lie*—Usage: confused word pair (lie/lay) **[4.8]**
3. *close together on*—Content: see caption (Acceptable: *together on*, etc.) **[2.1]**

4. *Paddling is*—Grammar: linking verb [**3.27**]

5. you *have* paddled—Grammar: helping verb (in present perfect tense) [**3.26, 3.24**]

6. *wave,*—Punctuation: comma used after introductory phrase [**5.15**]

7. *fast*—Grammar: adverb modifies verb [**3.4**]

8. *push. When*—Punctuation: run-on sentence [**5.37**]

9. *steady and*—Punctuation: sentence fragment [**5.38**]

10. *slightly forward*—Content: see caption [**2.1**]

How to Catch a Wave Corrected

The first steps in learning how to surf are balancing on the surfboard and paddling. To begin, lie horizontally along the center of the board. To balance, place your feet close together on the board. Paddling is done with alternating left and right strokes. After you have paddled out, you should face the ocean and start looking for a wave. When you see a good wave, turn yourself and your board towards the beach and begin paddling as strong and fast as you can. Arch your back to keep the nose of your board from going underwater, and the wave will give you a nice push. When you feel the force of the wave, you should lift yourself up and place your feet sideways on the board. Keep your board steady and just ahead of the breaking wave. Your knees should be bent, and your torso should be slightly forward. Now hang loose, and don't wipe out!

11. The Monarch

12 errors—1 content; 2 capitalization; 3 grammar; 3 punctuation; 2 spelling; 1 usage

The Monarch Errors

In the spring, butterflys[1] seem to be everywhere, but where do they live during the winter? In Autumn[2], flocks of [3]north american[3] monarch butterflies migrate south to milder climates. One of their destinations are[4] Pacific Grove, California[5] where they will remain until spring. They hibernate in trees in the parks and surrounding areas. In some areas, special butterfly habitats have been set aside to protect these weekly[6] visitors. When you visit these habitats, you see what look like large clusters of dried leafs[7] hanging from the trees. In fact, these clusters are hundreds of butterflies with their wings closed. The dull underpart of the monarch's wing.[8] Resembles a dead leaf and provides the butterfly with protective camouflage while it is rest[9]. The butterflies hang down in overlapping layers from the tree branches. They will hibernate this way until spring arrived[10]. When the butterflies[11] wings are warm[12] by the sun, they will begin to fly again.

1. *butterflies*—Spelling [**6.4**]

2. *autumn*—Capital: unnecessary [**1.8**]

3. *North American*—Capital: proper adjective [**1.4**]

4. *is*—Usage: agreement of verb with subject in number (one is) [**4.2**]

5. *California,*—Punctuation: comma used after state (city, state,) in sentence [**5.8**]

6. *yearly*—Content: see caption [**2.1**]

7. *leaves*—Spelling [**6.3**]

8. *wing resembles*—Punctuation: sentence fragment [**5.38**]

9. is *resting*—Grammar: present participle (in present progressive tense) (Acceptable: *at rest,* or it *rests*) [**3.22, 3.24, 3.25**]

10. *arrives*—Grammar: present tense verb [**3.24**]

11. *butterflies'*—Punctuation: apostrophe with possessive of plural ending in *s* [**5.3**]

12. *warmed*—Grammar: past participle verb (in present tense passive voice) [**3.22, 3.24, 3.25**]

The Monarch Corrected

In the spring, butterflies seem to be everywhere, but where do they live during the winter? In autumn, flocks of North American monarch butterflies migrate south to milder climates. One of their destinations is Pacific Grove, California, where they will remain until spring. They hibernate in trees in the parks and surrounding areas. In some areas, special butterfly habitats have been set aside to protect these yearly visitors. When you visit these habitats, you see what look like large clusters of dried leaves hanging from the trees. In fact, these clusters are hundreds of butterflies with their wings closed. The dull underpart of the monarch's wing resembles a dead leaf and provides the butterfly with protective camouflage while it is resting. The butterflies hang down in overlapping layers from the tree branches. They will hibernate this way until spring arrives. When the butterflies' wings are warmed by the sun, they will begin to fly again.

12. Drumming It In

12 errors—1 content; 2 capitalization; 2 grammar; 4 punctuation; 1 spelling; 2 usage

Drumming It In Errors

Most of my drumming moves was[1] okay, but I wanted to get even better. I was pretty excited when my instructor showed up at 430[2]. "Hey, professor[3], I'm so glad you came to learn[4] me to play!" I said. He got to the point. "Let's see how you play now, and then we'll improve it," he said. I played [5]Tapper's Suite[5] better than ever, but my skill went unnoticed. "First," he said, "You[6] must set the drum at elbow level. Then we'll worked[7] on your arms and hands." We positioned the drum, and I played again. "Your left hand[8] your weaker[8] is lagging," he said, "and, what's worse, your[9] holding the stick wrong." He made me hold my elbows in[10] [11] grip the

sticks securely, and strike with the same force from each hand. I was happier before I knew how worse[12] I was.

1. *were*—Usage: agreement of verb with indefinite pronoun (most/were) **[4.4]**
2. *4:30*—Punctuation: colon with hours and minutes **[5.4]**
3. *Professor*—Capital: title used as proper name **[1.6]**
4. *teach*—Usage: confused word pair (learn/teach) **[4.8]**
5. *"Tapper's Suite"*—Punctuation: quotation marks with title of song **[5.32]**
6. *"you*—Capital: unnecessary (divided quotation) **[1.2]**
7. *work*—Grammar: infinitive (used in future tense verb) **[3.22, 3.24]**
8. *hand, your weaker,*—Punctuation: comma with nonessential appositive **[5.16]**
9. *you're*—Spelling **[6.1]**
10. *elbows out*—Content: see illustration and caption **[2.1]**
11. *out,*—Punctuation: commas used after phrases in a series **[5.6]**
12. *bad*—Grammar: positive adjective (not comparative) **[3.1]**

Drumming It In Corrected

Most of my drumming moves were okay, but I wanted to get even better. I was pretty excited when my instructor showed up at 4:30. "Hey, Professor, I'm so glad you came to teach me to play!" I said. He got to the point. "Let's see how you play now, and then we'll improve it," he said. I played "Tapper's Suite" better than ever, but my skill went unnoticed. "First," he said, "you must set the drum at elbow level. Then we'll work on your arms and hands." We positioned the drum, and I played again. "Your left hand, your weaker, is lagging," he said, "and, what's worse, you're holding the stick wrong." He made me hold my elbows out, grip the sticks securely, and strike with the same force from each hand. I was happier before I knew how bad I was.

13. Spiders and Crabs

11 errors—2 content; 2 grammar; 2 punctuation; 5 usage

Spiders and Crabs Errors

Spiders and crabs can look very similar and are, in fact, both classify[1] as arthropods. Arthropods are invertebrate animals that have jointed legs and segmented bodies. Both a spider and a crab has[2] two main body section[3], the cephalothorax and the abdomen. The cephalothorax is a combined head and chest to which the legs are attach[4]. The spider has [5]ten legs, and the crab has eight[5]. All arthropods also have inner[6] shells called exoskeletons that protect and support its[7] bodies, improve locomotion, and shed periodically as they grow [8]and crabs have compound eyes that consist of many lenses, but spiders[9] eyes have only one lens each. Unlike other types of arthropods, spiders don't have no[10] antennae. However, crabs usually have two pairs of antennae on their heads. The crabs use this[11] antennae as sense organs.

1. *classified*—Grammar: past participle (in present tense passive voice) **[3.22, 3.24, 3.25]**
2. *have*—Usage: agreement of verb with compound subject **[4.3]**
3. *sections*—Usage: agreement of noun with adjective in number **[4.5]**
4. are *attached*—Grammar: past participle (in present tense passive voice) **[3.22, 3.24, 3.25]**
5. spider has *eight...ten*—Content: see illustration **[2.1]**
6. *outer* shells—Content: see caption **[2.1]**
7. *their* bodies—Usage: agreement of pronoun with noun **[4.1]**
8. grow. ~~and~~ Crabs—Punctuation: run-on sentence **[5.37]**
9. *spiders'* eyes—Punctuation: apostrophe with possessive of plural **[5.3]**
10. don't have ~~no~~ antennae—Usage:

double negative (Acceptable: *spiders have no antennae*) **[4.7]**
11. *these* antennae—Usage: agreement of demonstrative adjective with noun **[4.5]**

Spiders and Crabs Corrected

Spiders and crabs can look very similar and are, in fact, both classified as arthropods. Arthropods are invertebrate animals that have jointed legs and segmented bodies. Both a spider and a crab have two main body sections, the cephalothorax and the abdomen. The cephalothorax is a combined head and chest to which the legs are attached. The spider has eight legs, and the crab has ten. All arthropods also have outer shells called exoskeletons that protect and support their bodies, improve locomotion, and shed periodically as they grow. Crabs have compound eyes that consist of many lenses, but spiders' eyes have only one lens each. Unlike other types of arthropods, spiders have no antennae. However, crabs usually have two pairs of antennae on their heads. The crabs use these antennae as sense organs.

14. The Giant of His Age

9 errors—1 content; 5 grammar; 2 punctuation; 1 usage

The Giant of His Age Errors

Leonardo da Vinci was a painter, a sculptor, a mathematician, a scientist, an engineer, a philosopher, and many other things. He was knowed[1] in popular culture for his paintings[2] including many that are still widely recognized. His most famous painting was the Whistler's Mother[3]. He was known for providing early models of technological advances that included the airplane, the automobile, and the parachute[4] he also proposes[5] using simple machines, such as pulleys and levers, to do complex tasks. One of his ideas were[6] the wheel-driven machine, which would use the turning of a wheel to produce energy. In addition, Leonardo [7]famous for his enormous number of drawings of the human body, including illustrations of the functions of bones and organs. His drawings were considered to be the first accurate portrayals of human anatomy. Because of the many contributions to ours[8] progress, Leonardo was a man to who[9] we owe many thanks.

1. was *known*—Grammar: past participle (in past tense passive voice) **[3.22, 3.24, 3.25]**
2. *paintings, including*—Punctuation: comma with nonessential appositive **[5.16]**
3. *Mona Lisa*—Content: see illustration and caption **[2.1]**
4. *parachute. He*—Punctuation: run-on sentence **[5.37]**
5. *proposed*—Grammar: past tense verb **[3.24]**
6. *was* the—Usage: agreement of verb with subject in number (one/was) **[4.2]**
7. Leonardo *was*—Grammar: linking verb (past tense) **[3.27]**
8. *our*—Grammar: possessive pronoun with noun **[3.19]**
9. to *whom*—Grammar: pronoun *whom* as object **[3.21]**

The Giant of His Age Corrected

Leonardo da Vinci was a painter, a sculptor, a mathematician, a scientist, an engineer, a philosopher, and many other things. He was known in popular culture for his paintings, including many that are still widely recognized. His most famous painting was the Mona Lisa. He was known for providing early models of technological advances that included the airplane, the automobile, and the parachute. He also proposed using simple machines, such as pulleys and levers, to do complex tasks. One of his ideas was the wheel-driven machine, which would use the turning of a wheel to produce energy. In addition, Leonardo was famous for his enormous number of drawings of the human body, including illustrations of the functions of bones and organs. His drawings were considered to be the first accurate portrayals of human anatomy. Because of the many contributions to our progress, Leonardo was a man to whom we owe many thanks.

15. Night Fright

12 errors—1 content; 2 capitalization; 3 grammar; 6 punctuation

Night Fright Errors

Deep in the night, she hears[1] the sound of water roaring through the hallway. Saraya peeked out her door. The hallway was as dry as it [2]been since she arrived earlier that day. It was even deeper in the night.[3] When she heard the horrible scream. She called out, and her voice echoed in the silence. It was almost morning when she felt her bed shake. She jumped up, threw open the door, and ran into the hall. Trying to ignore the intensifying screech behind her, she zoomed.[4] Down the long stairway,[5] and into the courtyard. She considered climbing over the wall that surrounded the castle but decided against it. Frantic, she ran along the wall until she stumbled and fell. She heard the noises right behind her and turned around to face hers[6] fate[7] and behind her, her brother was smiling and holding a CD player that was playing "Sounds in the night[8]." "That's not fair[9] Mohammed.[10]" Saraya cried. Mohammed just laughed. "We'll leave tomorrow. You'll see," Saraya said, planning to ask [11]mom and dad[11] to cut the visit [12]in half[12].

1. *heard*—Grammar: past tense verb **[3.24]**
2. *had* been—Grammar: helping verb (in past perfect tense) **[3.26, 3.24]**
3. *night when*—Punctuation: sentence fragment **[5.38]**

4. *zoomed down*—Punctuation: sentence fragment **[5.38]**

5. *stairway and*—Punctuation: unnecessary comma **[5.21]**

6. *her* fate—Grammar: possessive pronoun with noun **[3.19]**

7. *fate. Behind*—Punctuation: run-on sentence **[5.37]**

8. *Night."*—Capital: song title **[1.9]**

9. *fair, Mohammed*—Punctuation: comma with noun of address **[5.13]**

10. *Mohammed!"*—Punctuation: exclamation mark in quoted exclamatory sentence **[5.22, 5.24]**

11. *Mom and Dad*—Capital: words used as proper names **[1.7]**

12. visit *short*—Content: see caption (Acceptable: *down*, to *shorten* the visit, etc.) **[2.1]**

Night Fright Corrected

Deep in the night, she heard the sound of water roaring through the hallway. Saraya peeked out her door. The hallway was as dry as it had been since she arrived earlier that day. It was even deeper in the night when she heard the horrible scream. She called out, and her voice echoed in the silence. It was almost morning when she felt her bed shake. She jumped up, threw open the door, and ran into the hall. Trying to ignore the intensifying screech behind her, she zoomed down the long stairway and into the courtyard. She considered climbing over the wall that surrounded the castle but decided against it. Frantic, she ran along the wall until she stumbled and fell. She heard the noises right behind her and turned around to face her fate. Behind her, her brother was smiling and holding a CD player that was playing "Sounds in the Night." "That's not fair, Mohammed!" Saraya cried. Mohammed just laughed. "We'll leave tomorrow. You'll see," Saraya said, planning to ask Mom and Dad to cut the visit short.

16. A Net Gain

11 errors—2 content; 1 grammar; 7 punctuation; 1 usage

A Net Gain Errors

In a stunning upset in the National Junior Tennis Championships, Marie O'Neal defeated heavy[1] favored Alicia Alfonso. O'Neal upset two other favored players.[2] On the way to her first national crown. In the title match, she lost her serve only in the last game of the second set. Alfonsos[3] serve[4] in contrast[4] was broken once in the first set and once in the third set[5] and she had not lost her serve in the previous three matches. O'Neal was happy that her hard work paid off. "This makes me very proud",[6] she said, [7]and I hope to do as well next year." Alfonso thought his[8] opponent deserved to win and said, "Marie played very well today. She kept the ball deep,[9] and won the big points. She has a tough lefty[10] serve." O'Neal planned to take some time off to enjoy her big win. Alfonso planned to return to her Columbus[11] home to continue training. Both players will try to qualify for the U.S. Open later this year.

1. *heavily*—Grammar: adverb used to modify adjective **[3.4]**

2. *players on*—Punctuation: sentence fragment **[5.38]**

3. *Alfonso's*—Punctuation: apostrophe in singular possessive **[5.3]**

4. *serve, in contrast,*—Punctuation: commas with sentence interrupters **[5.17]**

5. *set. She*—Punctuation: run-on sentence **[5.37]**

6. *proud,"*—Punctuation: comma inside quotation marks **[5.20]**

7. *"and*—Punctuation: quotation marks enclose both parts of divided quotation **[5.31]**

8. *her*—Usage: agreement of pronoun with noun in gender **[4.1]**

9. *deep and*—Punctuation: unnecessary comma **[5.21]**
10. *right-handed* serve—Content: see picture (Acceptable: *righty*, etc. Note: students at this level may not know about hypnenation of adjectives) **[2.1]**
11. *Cincinnati*—Content: see caption **[2.1]**

A Net Gain Corrected

In a stunning upset in the National Junior Tennis Championships, Marie O'Neal defeated heavily favored Alicia Alfonso. O'Neal upset two other favored players on the way to her first national crown. In the title match, she lost her serve only in the last game of the second set. Alfonso's serve, in contrast, was broken once in the first set and once in the third set. She had not lost her serve in the previous three matches. O'Neal was happy that her hard work paid off. "This makes me very proud," she said, "and I hope to do as well next year." Alfonso thought her opponent deserved to win and said, "Marie played very well today. She kept the ball deep and won the big points. She has a tough right-handed serve." O'Neal planned to take some time off to enjoy her big win. Alfonso planned to return to her Cincinnati home to continue training. Both players will try to qualify for the U.S. Open later this year.

17. A Glimpse into the Past

11 errors—3 content; 2 capitalization; 2 grammar; 4 punctuation

A Glimpse into the Past Errors

Tucson, Arizona
January 29, 2001

Dear Linda[1]
I haven't written since my letter of December 22, 2000[2] because I've been busy writing a report about Machu Picchu. This hidden city is 8,000 feet high and was built by the Incas in South Africa[3]. The Incas were conquered in the 1500s, but many of them fled to this secret city. It remained

undiscovered for about another 500[4] years. I read and am sending you "Secrets of the [5]past," an article that gives many facts about the ruins. As you can see, it shows a stone wall with a man who is only half[6] as tall. I also read [7]Inca Treasures[7], a story about a[8] Inca man. I liked the story but learned more from the article. Both gave me a glimpse of the world of the Incas. Their lives were far different from our[9] in Tucson, Arizona[10] today!

Your [11]Friend,
Azzi

1. *Linda,*—Punctuation: comma used after greeting of friendly letter **[5.11]**
2. *2000,* because—Punctuation: comma after year in sentence (*month day, year,*) **[5.10]**
3. *South America*—Content: see illustration **[2.1]**
4. *400*—Content: see caption **[2.1]**
5. *"Secrets of the Past,"*—Capital: first and last words in article title **[1.9]**
6. *a third*—Content: see illustration (Acceptable: *one-third, 1/3*, etc.) **[2.1]**
7. *"Inca Treasures,"*—Punctuation: quotation marks with story title **[5.32]**
8. *an Inca*—Grammar: article *an* before vowel sound **[3.5]**
9. *ours*—Grammar: possessive pronoun without noun **[3.19]**
10. *Arizona,*—Punctuation: comma used after state (city, state,) in sentence **[5.8]**
11. *friend*—Capital: only first word in closing of friendly letter **[1.11]**

A Glimpse into the Past Corrected

Tucson, Arizona
January 29, 2001

Dear Linda,
I haven't written since my letter of December 22, 2000, because I've been busy writing a report about Machu Picchu. This hidden city is 8,000 feet high and was built by the Incas in South America. The Incas were conquered in the 1500s, but many of them fled to this secret

city. It remained undiscovered for about another 400 years. I read and am sending you "Secrets of the Past," an article that gives many facts about the ruins. As you can see, it shows a stone wall with a man who is only a third as tall. I also read "Inca Treasures," a story about an Inca man. I liked the story but learned more from the article. Both gave me a glimpse of the world of the Incas. Their lives were far different from ours in Tucson, Arizona, today!

Your friend,
Azzi

18. A Sucker for Squid

10 errors—2 content; 1 grammar; 4 punctuation; 1 spelling; 2 usage

A Sucker for Squid Errors

A hidden video camera finally captured the thief whod[1] been stealing the octopus food. Over the last few days[2] a lab assistant had noticed something strange. [3]Pieces of squid were missing from the jar of food each morning[3] kept near the octopus tank. He set up a hidden video camera.[4] To monitor the lab one night. The next day, the mystery was solved. The octopus had found a small opening in the cover of its tank. During the night, it would squeeze through the opening. Like all octopuses, it was able to compress all of it's[5] body except the back[6]. Fortunately for the octopus, the opening were[7] large enough for the mouth to fit through. Sliding its tentacles through first, it had pulled the rest of its body through the opening. Using the suckers on its legs[8], the octopus had then grasped the lid of the jar, pulls[9] it off[10] removed a piece of squid, and proceeded to snack. When it was done eating, the octopus had climbed back inside the tank.

1. *who'd*—Punctuation: apostrophe in contraction [5.1]
2. *days,*—Punctuation: comma used after introductory phrase [5.15]
3. *Each morning, pieces of squid were missing from the jar of food…*—Usage: misplaced modifier (Acceptable: *Pieces of squid were missing each morning from the jar of food…*) [4.6]
4. *camera to*—Punctuation: sentence fragment [5.38]
5. *its*—Spelling [6.1]
6. *mouth*—Content: see caption (Acceptable: *beak*) [2.1]
7. opening *was*—Usage: agreement of verb with subject in number [4.2]
8. *arms*—Content: see illustration and caption [2.1]
9. *pulled*—Grammar: past tense verb [3.24]
10. *off,*—Punctuation: comma used after phrases in a series [5.6]

A Sucker for Squid Corrected

A hidden video camera finally captured the thief who'd been stealing the octopus food. Over the last few days, a lab assistant had noticed something strange. Each morning, pieces of squid were missing from the jar of food kept near the octopus tank. He set up a hidden video camera to monitor the lab one night. The next day, the mystery was solved. The octopus had found a small opening in the cover of its tank. During the night, it would squeeze through the opening. Like all octopuses, it was able to compress all of its body except the mouth. Fortunately for the octopus, the opening was large enough for the mouth to fit through. Sliding its tentacles through first, it had pulled the rest of its body through the opening. Using the suckers on its arms, the octopus had then grasped the lid of the jar, pulled it off, removed a piece of squid, and proceeded to snack. When it was done eating, the octopus had climbed back inside the tank.

19. The Eagle Nebula

12 errors—2 content; 2 grammar; 6 punctuation; 2 usage

The Eagle Nebula Errors

As I clicked through the television channels, my favorite science show appeared. "The Hubble Space Telescope[1] launched in 1990, has recorded.[2] Many astounding images for we[3] earthbound humans",[4] the announcer was saying. "One such image is this picture of the Eagle Nebula, outside[5] the Milky Way galaxy".[6] A brilliant vision of the nebula filled my screen as he continued. "Radiation from nearby stars cause[7] these enormous towers of gas and dust to glow,[8] notice the globules of gas at the top of the rightmost[9] tower. Each glob may contain new[10] forming stars and are[11] about the size of our solar system!" Wow! Where else could I learn as much as I do from "Outer Visions?"[12]

1. *Telescope,* —Punctuation: comma with nonessential appositive **[5.16]**
2. *recorded many*—Punctuation: sentence fragment **[5.38]**
3. *us*—Grammar: pronoun as object **[3.19]**
4. *humans,"*—Punctuation: comma inside quotation marks **[5.20]**
5. *inside*—Content: see caption **[2.1]**
6. *galaxy."*—Punctuation: period inside quotation marks **[5.28]**
7. *causes*—Usage: agreement of verb with subject in number (radiation/causes) **[4.2]**
8. *glow. Notice*—Punctuation: run-on sentence (Acceptable: *glow; notice*) **[5.37]**
9. *leftmost*—Content: see illustration **[2.1]**
10. *newly*—Grammar: adverb modifies adjective **[3.4]**
11. *is*—Usage: agreement of verb with subject in number (glob/is) **[4.2]**
12. *Visions"?*—Punctuation: question mark outside quotation marks when it doesn't apply to material in quotation marks **[5.30]**

The Eagle Nebula Corrected

As I clicked through the television channels, my favorite science show appeared. "The Hubble Space Telescope, launched in 1990, has recorded many astounding images for us earthbound humans," the announcer was saying. "One such image is this picture of the Eagle Nebula, inside the Milky Way galaxy." A brilliant vision of the nebula filled my screen as he continued. "Radiation from nearby stars causes these enormous towers of gas and dust to glow. Notice the globules of gas at the top of the leftmost tower. Each glob may contain newly forming stars and is about the size of our solar system!" Wow! Where else could I learn as much as I do from "Outer Visions"?

20. Deadly Dino

11 errors—2 content; 1 capitalization; 2 grammar; 4 punctuation; 1 spelling; 1 usage

Deadly Dino Errors

Tyrannosaurus rex was the most feared predator of it's[1] time. It could run very fast on its powerful hind legs[2] and its sharp teeth were effective in catching its food[3] and *Tyrannosaurus rex* and other dinosaurs first appeared about 200 million years ago. They became extinct.[4] About 65 million years ago. For more than 135 million years, dinosaurs ruled the world. *Tyrannosaurus rex* was the King[5] of them all. The T-rex, as it are[6] popularly called, had two long hind legs that it used for walking or running and two longer[7] front legs that it used for attacking its prey. Even at 20 feet tall[8] the T-rex was not the taller[9] of all dinosaurs. That was a[10] honor belonging to *Brachiosaurus*, which could have looked over a building three stories high. The ability to [11]reach tall plants for food[11] made T-rex the most feared predator of prehistoric times.

1. *its*—Spelling **[6.1]**
2. *legs,* and—Punctuation: comma used before coordinating conjunctions

joining independent clauses [5.18, 5.33]

3. *food. Tyrannosaurus*—Punctuation: run-on sentence [5.37]

4. *extinct about*—Punctuation: sentence fragment [5.38]

5. *king*—Capital: unnecessary [1.6]

6. *is*—Usage: agreement of verb with subject in number (in adjective clause) [4.2]

7. *shorter*—Content: see illustration [2.1]

8. *tall,*—Punctuation: comma used after introductory phrase [5.15]

9. *tallest*—Grammar: superlative adjective [3.9]

10. *an honor*—Grammar: article *an* before vowel sound [3.5]

11. *catch and eat other dinosaurs*—Content: see caption and illustration (Acceptable: *run down other dinosaurs*, etc.) [2.1]

Deadly Dino Corrected

Tyrannosaurus rex was the most feared predator of its time. It could run very fast on its powerful hind legs, and its sharp teeth were effective in catching its food. *Tyrannosaurus rex* and other dinosaurs first appeared about 200 million years ago. They became extinct about 65 million years ago. For more than 135 million years, dinosaurs ruled the world. *Tyrannosaurus rex* was the king of them all. The T-rex, as it is popularly called, had two long hind legs that it used for walking or running and two shorter front legs that it used for attacking its prey. Even at 20 feet tall, the T-rex was not the tallest of all dinosaurs. That was an honor belonging to *Brachiosaurus*, which could have looked over a building three stories high. The ability to catch and eat other dinosaurs made T-rex the most feared predator of prehistoric times.

21. Victory on Wheels

12 errors—2 content; 1 capitalization; 3 grammar; 6 punctuation;

Victory on Wheels Errors

Amy was fast that day. In fact, she had never rode[1] faster. "she[2] rides like the wind[3]" her husband said as she whizzed by. She had been trailing[4] the pack by more than 30 seconds. She thrust her fists in the air and yelled excitedly as she came across the finish line twenty:[5]six[6] seconds before the next finisher. It was her second victory in a bicycle race. She and her husband tried to decide what contributed to her great finish. "Was it what I ate"?[7] she asked. "Maybe it was because you were well rested,[8] he said. They decided that her success was probably a combination of all the possibilities[9] and that made it difficult to duplicate. Anyway, victory is[10] her[11]. Amy's mind was already racing to the womens'[12] triathlon that would take place in three weeks. Would she make it her next victory?

1. had never *ridden*—Grammar: irregular past participle (in past perfect tense) [3.22, 3.24, 3.25]

2. *"She*—Capital: first word in a quotation [1.2]

3. *wind,"*—Punctuation: comma separates direct quote from speaker [5.19]

4. *leading*—Content: see caption [2.1]

5. *twenty-two*—Punctuation: hyphen used in compound number [5.25]

6. twenty-*two*—Content: see caption (48 min 45 sec from 49 min 7 sec. = 22 seconds) [2.1]

7. *ate?"*—Punctuation: question mark inside quotation marks when it applies to quoted material [5.30]

8. *rested,"*—Punctuation: quotation marks enclose a direct quote [5.31]

9. *possibilities,* and—Punctuation: comma used before coordinating conjunction joining independent clauses [5.18, 5.33]

10. *was*—Grammar: linking verb (past tense) **[3.27]**
11. *hers*—Grammar: possessive pronoun without noun **[3.19]**
12. *women's*—Punctuation: apostrophe with possessive of plural not beginning with *s* **[5.3]**

Victory on Wheels Corrected

Amy was fast that day. In fact, she had never ridden faster. "She rides like the wind," her husband said as she whizzed by. She had been leading the pack by more than 30 seconds. She thrust her fists in the air and yelled excitedly as she came across the finish line twenty-two seconds before the next finisher. It was her first victory in a bicycle race. She and her husband tried to decide what contributed to her great finish. "Was it what I ate?" she asked. "Maybe it was because you were well rested," he said. They decided that her success was probably a combination of all the possibilities, and that made it difficult to duplicate. Anyway, victory was hers. Amy's mind was already racing to the women's triathlon that would take place in three weeks. Would she make it her next victory?

22. An Archaeological Find

10 errors—1 content; 4 grammar; 3 punctuation; 1 spelling; 1 usage

An Archaeological Find Errors

Today, our exacting field work in Australia was reward[1]. We spended[2] most of the day carefully uncovering what seemed to be an ancient knife. We had many questions. When was it made? Was it used as a weapon? Was it used for cooking? Once the knife [3]uncovered, we noticed another object just below it. It was a small wood carving in the shape of a dingo, a dog brought to Australia by the Aborigines about 5000 to 8000 years ago. We theorized that the knife was most likely used to carve the wooden dog. However[4] we had no indication of the carvings[5] age. We will had[6] to use the tree ring dating method to find out how old the carving actually is. Every wooden object has tree rings. Each ring represents one year of growth. We will compare the rings of the carving to the rings of a faraway[7] tree to see were[8] they match[9] and we are eager to find out how old this[10] artifacts really are. What more will we discover?

1. *rewarded*—Grammar: past participle (in past tense passive voice) **[3.22, 3.24, 3.25]**
2. *spent*—Grammar: past tense verb **[3.24]**
3. *was* uncovered—Grammar: helping verb (in past tense passive voice) **[3.26, 3.24]**
4. *However,*—Punctuation: comma used after introductory word **[5.14]**
5. *carving's*—Punctuation: apostrophe with singular possessive **[5.3]**
6. *have*—Grammar: infinitive with future tense verb **[3.22, 3.24]**
7. *nearby*—Content: see illustration **[2.1]**
8. *where*—Spelling **[6.1]**
9. *match. We*—Punctuation—run-on sentence **[5.37]**
10. *these*—Usage: agreement of demonstrative adjective with noun **[4.5]**

An Archaeological Find Corrected

Today, our exacting field work in Australia was rewarded. We spent most of the day carefully uncovering what seemed to be an ancient knife. We had many questions. When was it made? Was it used as a weapon? Was it used for cooking? Once the knife was uncovered, we noticed another object just below it. It was a small wood carving in the shape of a dingo, a dog brought to Australia by the Aborigines about 5000 to 8000 years ago. We theorized that the knife was most likely used to carve the wooden dog. However, we had no indication of the carving's age. We will have to use the tree ring dating method to find out how old the carving actually is.

Every wooden object has tree rings. Each ring represents one year of growth. We will compare the rings of the carving to the rings of a nearby tree to see where they match. We are eager to find out how old these artifacts really are. What more will we discover?

23. An Early American

13 errors—2 content; 1 capitalization; 2 grammar; 4 punctuation; 1 spelling; 3 usage

An Early American Errors

We could hardly wait to hear the author of "Early Americanimals!"[1] "Had you lived during the 1830s[2] you might have seen great herds of bison grazing between the Appalachian Mountains and the Rockies," he began. "Though many of these majestic creatures were wiped out, some is[3] around today." We interrupted him. "How would you know a pair of bison if themselves[4] walked down your street?" we asked. "Well," he answered, "Most[5] bisons'[6] hair is coarse and brown. Each have[7] a hump on the back. Three[8] horns adorn each massive head, and the bison wear beards under their chins. A bull weighs close to a ton, but a cow weighs twice[9] as much. When provoked, each of the two bisons[10] could probably run quite fastly[11]. Let's hope that you would run the faster[12] [13]"! We were glad that our hero had both knowledge and a sense of humor.

1. *Americanimals"!*—Punctuation: exclamation mark outside quotation marks (it applies to entire sentence) **[5.24, 5.22]**
2. *1830s,*—Punctuation: comma used after introductory dependent clause **[5.15]**
3. some *are*—Usage: agreement of verb with indefinite pronoun **[4.4]**
4. if *they*—Usage: pronoun as subject (not reflexive) **[3.19, 3.20]**
5. *"most*—Capital: unnecessary (divided quotation) **[1.2]**

6. *bison's*—Punctuation: apostrophe with possessive of plural not ending in *s* **[5.3]**
7. each *has*—Usage: agreement of verb with indefinite pronoun **[4.4]**
8. *Two* horns—Content: see illustration **[2.1]**
9. *half*—Content: see caption **[2.1]**
10. *bison*—Spelling (plural form) **[6.2]**
11. *fast*—Grammar: adverb used to modify verb **[3.4]**
12. *fastest*—Grammar: superlative adverb **[3.9]**
13. *fastest!"*—Punctuation: exclamation mark inside quotation marks when it applies to material inside quote **[5.24]**

An Early American Corrected

We could hardly wait to hear the author of "Early Americanimals"! "Had you lived during the 1830s, you might have seen great herds of bison grazing between the Appalachian Mountains and the Rockies," he began. "Though many of these majestic creatures were wiped out, some are around today." We interrupted him. "How would you know a pair of bison if they walked down your street?" we asked. "Well," he answered, "most bison's hair is coarse and brown. Each has a hump on the back. Two horns adorn each massive head, and the bison wear beards under their chins. A bull weighs close to a ton, but a cow weighs half as much. When provoked, each of the two bison could probably run quite fast. Let's hope that you would run the fastest!" We were glad that our hero had both knowledge and a sense of humor.

24. A Profitable Platform

11 errors—1 content; 6 grammar; 2 punctuation; 2 usage

A Profitable Platform Errors

Dear Editor:

As part of my campaign platform for student body president, I would like to propose that students be paid for attending school. My mom is always telling me that school is my job. Students would learn much fast[1] than usual if they got paid for it, and they would get valuable experience in earning a living. If I had been pay[2] $5.00 for each hour I attended school last semester, I would have earned a whole lot more than I did. Instead[3] my parents paid me only $11.00[4] for the two A's that I got on my report card last semester. [5]The thing is is[5] the school could establish a salary scale that was base[6] on letter grades and pay each of us students an hourly wage based on their[7] previous semester's academic performance. My[8] would sure[9] improve. I hope the school administration will give my request due consideration and that the students [10]be able to vote on this important issue.

Sincerely:[11]
Justin Case

1. *faster*—Grammar: comparative adverb **[3.9]**
2. been *paid*—Grammar: past participle (in past perfect tense) **[3.22, 3.24, 3.25]**
3. *Instead,* my—Punctuation: comma used after introductory word **[5.14]**
4. *$10.00*—Content: see caption **[2.1]**
5. *The school could*—Usage: unnecessary words (Acceptable: *The thing is that the school…*) **[4.7]**
6. was *based*—Grammar: past participle (in past tense passive voice) **[3.22, 3.24, 3.25]**
7. *our* academic—Usage: agreement of pronoun with noun in person **[4.1]**
8. *Mine*—Grammar: possessive pronoun without noun (Acceptable: *My performance, My grades*, etc.) **[3.19]**
9. *surely*—Grammar: adverb modifies verb **[3.4]**
10. *will* be able—Grammar: helping verb (in future perfect tense) **[3.26, 3.24]**
11. *Sincerely,*—Punctuation: comma after closing of letter **[5.12]**

A Profitable Platform Corrected

Dear Editor:

As part of my campaign platform for student body president, I would like to propose that students be paid for attending school. My mom is always telling me that school is my job. Students would learn much faster than usual if they got paid for it, and they would get valuable experience in earning a living. If I had been paid $5.00 for each hour I attended school last semester, I would have earned a whole lot more than I did. Instead, my parents paid me only $10.00 for the two A's that I got on my report card last semester. The school could establish a salary scale that was based on letter grades and pay each of us students an hourly wage based on our previous semester's academic performance. Mine would surely improve. I hope the school administration will give my request due consideration and that the students will be able to vote on this important issue.

Sincerely,
Justin Case

25. Heart-Racing Journey

12 errors—2 content; 6 grammar; 1 punctuation; 3 spelling

Heart-Racing Journey Errors

With the goal of studying a microscopic society, I prepare for transport. I am successfully shrinked[1], but something [2]gone wrong with the coordinates! I materialize in the right atrium of a chambered muscular organ. What could of[3] happened? Suddenly, all is still, and I brace for a contraction. The jolt hurls the blood cells and I[4] past the mitral[5] valve into the right ventricle. Hey[6] I have somehow survived! The ventricle squeezes the blood and myself[7] toward the lungs, were[8] I can be saved. Our engineer will surely locate and beam me out once I'm there. I am propelled with a rush but slow down just at the pulmonary valve. Its two[9] cusps trap myself[10] like doors as me[11] struggle to get out! I am not to be defeated, though. With a mighty effort, I pull my hips through and then my legs, to[12]. I am free of the heart! I glide to the lungs, sure that I will soon be saved.

1. *shrunk*—Grammar: past participle (in present tense passive voice **[3.22, 3.24, 3.25]**
2. *has* gone—Grammar: helping verb (in present perfect tense) **[3.26, 3.24]**
3. could *have*—Spelling/usage **[6.5]**
4. cells and *me*—Grammar: pronoun as object **[3.19]**
5. *tricuspid*—Content: see illustration (Acceptable: past the *right atrium* into) **[2.1]**
6. *Hey,*—Punctuation: comma after interjection **[5.14]**
7. blood and *me*—Grammar: pronoun as object (not reflexive) **[3.19, 3.20]**
8. *where*—Spelling **[6.1]**
9. *three*—Content: see illustration **[2.1]**
10. *me*—Grammar: pronoun as object (not reflexive) **[3.19, 3.20]**
11. *I* struggle—Grammar: pronoun as subject (in adverb clause) **[3.19]**
12. *too*—Spelling **[6.1]**

Heart-Racing Journey Corrected

With the goal of studying a microscopic society, I prepare for transport. I am successfully shrunk, but something has gone wrong with the coordinates! I materialize in the right atrium of a chambered muscular organ. What could have happened? Suddenly, all is still, and I brace for a contraction. The jolt hurls the blood cells and me past the tricuspid valve into the right ventricle. Hey, I have somehow survived! The ventricle squeezes the blood and me toward the lungs, where I can be saved. Our engineer will surely locate and beam me out once I'm there. I am propelled with a rush but slow down just at the pulmonary valve. Its three cusps trap me like doors as I struggle to get out! I am

not to be defeated, though. With a mighty effort, I pull my hips through and then my legs, too. I am free of the heart! I glide to the lungs, sure that I will soon be saved.

26. Schedule It!

Schedule It! Errors

13 errors—3 content; 1 capitalization; 3 grammar; 4 punctuation; 2 usage

Did she like being disorganized? Did she enjoy doing homework when her friends said, "Let's go dancing?"[1] No, she did not. On the other hand, she felt overwhelmed with things to do. Her father, whom[2] was a good advisor, came to the rescue with an article called [3]Doing It All".[4] He said, "Prioritize your activities, and then leave[5] go of the things that matter the less[6]. Schedule the important things first, and fit the other stuff around them." Soon, Juanita was penning[7] activities on her schedule. She managed to include at least one fun thing each day. On Thursdays, she would surf at 3[8]30 and watch her favorite television show [9]right after dinner[9]. Instead of arguing and playing with her brother after doing dishes, she would practice her music for [10]an hour[10]. She was pleased as she closed her eyes that night. "Tomorrow," Juanita said to himself[11], "Things[12] would[13] be different."

1. *dancing"?*—Punctuation: question mark outside quotation marks when it doesn't apply to quoted material **[5.30]**
2. *who*—Grammar: pronoun *who* as subject **[3.21]**
3. *"Doing It All"*—Punctuation: quotation marks enclose article title **[5.32]**
4. *All."*—Punctuation: period inside quotation marks **[5.28]**
5. *let* go—Usage: confused word pair (leave/let) **[4.8]**
6. *least*—Grammar: superlative adverb **[3.9]**
7. *penciling*—Content: see illustration

and caption **[2.1]**

8. *3:30*—Punctuation: colon separates hours and minutes **[5.4]**
9. *at 9:30*—Content: see illustration (Acceptable: *right after her reading assignment*, etc.) **[2.1]**
10. *45 minutes*—Content: see illustration **[2.1]**
11. *herself*—Usage: agreement of reflexive pronoun with antecedent **[4.1, 3.20]**
12. *"things*—Capital: unnecessary (divided quotation) **[1.2]**
13. *will*—Grammar: future tense verb **[3.24]**

Schedule It! Corrected

Did she like being disorganized? Did she enjoy doing homework when her friends said, "Let's go dancing"? No, she did not. On the other hand, she felt overwhelmed with things to do. Her father, who was a good advisor, came to the rescue with an article called "Doing It All." He said, "Prioritize your activities, and then let go of the things that matter the least. Schedule the important things first, and fit the other stuff around them." Soon, Juanita was penciling activities on her schedule. She managed to include at least one fun thing each day. On Thursdays, she would surf at 3:30 and watch her favorite television show at 9:30. Instead of arguing and playing with her brother after doing dishes, she would practice her music for 45 minutes. She was pleased as she closed her eyes that night. "Tomorrow," Juanita said to herself, "things will be different."

27. Bales of Fun

13 errors—2 content; 3 grammar: 5 punctuation; 3 usage

Bales of Fun Errors

Rural Route 1
Canton, NY,[1] 13617
June 11, 1998

Dear Pham[2]

I'll bet your city is very exciting, but, believe me[3] living in rural St[4] Lawrence County can be great. We are located northwest[5] of Lake Ontario between the Adirondack Mts[6] and [7]New York City[7]. [8]I and my sister[8] work here on our dairy farm every day. At milking time, I spread the straw while Cindy carries pails of milk. When we do the haying, Cindy picks up bales weighing a hundred pounds each and hoists them onto the wagon. [9]I drive the tractor pulling the wagon drinking iced tea[9]. At the barn, I watch the bales raise[10] to the loft on the hay elevator. I leave[11] Cindy have the honor of catching and neatly stacking the bales in the 100° heat of the barn. It's a great life for him[12] and I[13]! I don't understand why Cindy can't wait to go to college in the city.

Sincerely,
Manuel

1. *NY 13617*—Punctuation: comma unnecessary **[5.7]**
2. *Pham*—Punctuation: comma after greeting of friendly letter **[5.11]**
3. *me,*—Punctuation: comma with sentence interrupter **[5.17]**
4. *St.*—Punctuation: period after abbreviation **[5.27]**
5. *northeast*—Content: see map key and farm location **[2.1]**
6. Mts.—Punctuation: period after abbreviation (Acceptable: Mountains) **[5.27]**
7. *Canada*—Content: see map in illustration (Acceptable: the Canadian border) **[2.1]**
8. *My sister and I*—Grammar: first person last **[3.19]**
9. *Drinking iced tea, I drive the tractor pulling the wagon*—Usage: misplaced modifier (Acceptable: *I drink iced tea as I drive...wagon.*) **[4.6]**
10. *rise*—Usage: confused word pair (*raise/rise*) **[4.8]**
11. *let*—Grammar: confused word pair (*let/leave*) **[4.8]**

12. *her*—Usage: agreement of pronoun and noun in gender **[4.1]**

13. *her* and *me*—Grammar: pronoun as object **[3.19]**

Bales of Fun Corrected

Rural Route 1
Canton, NY 13617
June 11, 1998

Dear Pham,

I'll bet your city is very exciting, but, believe me, living in rural St. Lawrence County can be great. We are located northeast of Lake Ontario between the Adirondack Mts. and Canada. My sister and I work here on our dairy farm every day. At milking time, I spread the straw while Cindy carries pails of milk. When we do the haying, Cindy picks up bales weighing a hundred pounds each and hoists them onto the wagon. Drinking iced tea, I drive the tractor pulling the wagon. At the barn, I watch the bales rise to the loft on the hay elevator. I let Cindy have the honor of catching and neatly stacking the bales in the 100° heat of the barn. It's a great life for her and me! I don't understand why Cindy can't wait to go to college in the city.

Sincerely,
Manuel

28. A Lesson on Haiku

14 errors—2 content; 2 capitalization; 3 grammar; 6 punctuation;1 usage

A Lesson on Haiku Errors

"Is this a haiku poem[1] Mr. Zaluski asked the class. The student's[2] eyes scanned the poem in their literature books. "[3]how is a haiku poem arranged?" the teacher questions[4]. "A haiku poem has seventeen syllables. It's arranged in three line[5] of five, six[6], and five syllables each[7]" Roberto replied. "Excellent[8] Roberto. You [9]been doing your homework. The haiku is a traditional form of japanese[10] poetry that was developed in the 1700s[11] by a man named Basho. What do you notice about haiku"?[12] Mr. Zaluski asked. "It's simple," Shakira stated. "Yes, the haiku seems simple because there are few words. However, it is meant to express something much more[13]". Carmen rose to the challenge. "Maybe the poet is try[14] to express serenity. On the other hand, maybe the flower is meant to symbolize renewal of life." Mr. Zaluski smiled. His class was really catching on.

1. *poem?"*—Punctuation: question mark with quoted direct question **[5.29, 5.30]**

2. *students'*—Punctuation: apostrophe with possessive of plural ending in *s* **[5.3]**

3. *"How*—Capital: first word in a quotation **[1.2]**

4. *questioned*—Grammar: past tense verb **[3.24]**

5. *lines*—Usage: agreement of noun with adjective in number **[4.5]**

6. *seven*—Content: see middle line of poem in illustration **[2.1]**

7. *each,"*—Punctuation: comma separates direct quote from speaker **[5.19]**

8. *Excellent, Roberto*—Punctuation: comma with noun of address **[5.13]**

9. You *have* been—Grammar: helping verb (in present perfect tense) **[3.26, 3.24]**

10. *Japanese*—Capital: proper adjective **[1.4]**

11. *1600s*—Content: see caption (17th century includes the 1600s) **[2.1]**

12. *haiku?"*—Punctuation: question mark inside quotation marks when it applies to the material inside quote **[5.30]**

13. *more."*—Punctuation: period inside quotation marks **[5.28]**

14. *trying*—Grammar: present participle verb (in present progressive tense) **[3.22, 3.24, 3.25]**

A Lesson on Haiku Corrected

"Is this a haiku poem?" Mr. Zaluski

asked the class. The students' eyes scanned the poem in their literature books. "How is a haiku poem arranged?" the teacher questioned. "A haiku poem has seventeen syllables. It's arranged in three lines of five, seven, and five syllables each." Roberto replied. "Excellent, Roberto. You have been doing your homework. The haiku is a traditional form of Japanese poetry that was developed in the 1600s by a man named Basho. What do you notice about haiku?" Mr. Zaluski asked. "It's simple," Shakira stated. "Yes, the haiku seems simple because there are few words. However, it is meant to express something much more." Carmen rose to the challenge. "Maybe the poet is trying to express serenity. On the other hand, maybe the flower is meant to symbolize renewal of life." Mr. Zaluski smiled. His class was really catching on.

29. Eclipsed!

12 errors—3 content; 2 capitalization; 3 grammar; 3 punctuation; 1 usage

Eclipsed! Errors

Stargazers from all over the world converged near Hilo, Hawaii[1] during the full[2] Moon to view a partial[3] solar eclipse. They came to spend a chilly morning in the observatory atop the volcano Mauna Kea, which is nearly 14,000 feet tall. As the [4]Sun hid more and more of the Moon[4], the cheers began. When the eclipse were[5] total, the cheers became an[6] deafening roar. It was a rare totally[7] eclipse visible from the Northern and Western Hemispheres. Most eclipses can usually be seen only in the Southern Hemisphere. The location was a real plus for Gin-Wei Chang, a devoted Observer[8]. "I've seen five in a row now, and this one is the better[9] because I didn't have to travel so far"[10] she said. "Last time, I had to watch from an island in the indian[11] Ocean." For all their preparation and excitement, the observers had little time to enjoy the view.

The Sun's total disappearance, which began at 1107[12] A.M., lasted only 4 minutes.

1. *Hawaii,*—Punctuation: comma used after state (city, state,) in sentence **[5.8]**
2. *new*—Content: see caption and diagram **[2.1]**
3. *total*—Content: see caption **[2.1]**
4. *Moon hid more and more of the Sun*—Content: see caption **[2.1]**
5. *was*—Usage: agreement of verb with subject in number in adverb clause **[4.2]**
6. *a*—Grammar: article *a* before consonant sound **[3.5]**
7. *total*—Grammar: adjective used to modify noun **[3.1]**
8. *observer*—Capital: unnecessary **[1.6]**
9. *best*—Grammar: superlative adjective **[3.9]**
10. *far,"*—Punctuation: comma inside quotation marks **[5.20]**
11. *Indian*—Capital: proper noun **[1.3]**
12. *11:07*—Punctuation: colon used with hours and minutes **[5.4]**

Eclipsed! Corrected

Stargazers from all over the world converged near Hilo, Hawaii, during the new Moon to view a total solar eclipse. They came to spend a chilly morning in the observatory atop the volcano Mauna Kea, which is nearly 14,000 feet tall. As the Moon hid more and more of the Sun, the cheers began. When the eclipse was total, the cheers became a deafening roar. It was a rare total eclipse visible from the Northern and Western Hemispheres. Most eclipses can usually be seen only in the Southern Hemisphere. The location was a real plus for Gin-Wei Chang, a devoted observer. "I've seen five in a row now, and this one is the best because I didn't have to travel so far," she said. "Last time, I had to watch from an island in the Indian Ocean." For all their preparation and excitement, the observers had little time to enjoy the view. The Sun's total disappearance, which began at 11:07 A.M., lasted only 4 minutes.

30. Footnotes in Anatomy

13 errors—1 content; 3 grammar; 7 punctuation; 1 spelling; 1 usage

Footnotes in Anatomy Errors

"Next[1] we're going to discuss the human foot, which has 24[2] bones in all," said Mrs. Langdon. "They can be divided into three different kinds." As she pointed at the ankle[3] Mrs. Langdon said, "Can anyone give the name for the ankle bones[4]" Becky answered that they were the tarsals. "That's right," Mrs. Langdon said. "The foot has seven tarsal bones. What about the instep bones?[5] Miguel correctly identified them as the metatarsals. "That's right again," Mrs. Langdon said. "The foot has five metatarsal bones. Whom[6] knows what we call the bones in our toes?" Nobody knew, so Mrs. Langdon continued. "The toe bones are called phalanges. The foot have[7] fourteen phalanges. To[8] are in the big toe, and three are in each of the other four toes. Can anyone guess why the big toe had[9] one fewest[10] bone than the rest of the toes? Oh, there's the bell. Well[11] have to take up that subject on Monday. "[12]Have a great weekend"![13]

1. *Next,*—Punctuation: comma used after introductory word **[5.14]**
2. *26*—Content: see caption **[2.1]**
3. *ankle,*—Punctuation: comma used after introductory dependent clause **[5.15]**
4. *bones?"*—Punctuation: question mark after direct question **[5.29]**
5. *bones?"*—Punctuation: quotation marks enclose a direct quote **[5.31]**
6. *Who* knows—Grammar: pronoun *who* used as subject **[3.21]**
7. *has*—Usage: agreement of verb with subject in number **[4.2]**
8. *Two*—Spelling **[6.1]**
9. *has*—Grammar: present tense verb **[3.24]**
10. *fewer*—Grammar: comparative adjective **[3.9]**
11. *We'll*—Punctuation: apostrophe in contraction **[5.1]**
12. Monday. *Have*—Punctuation: unnecessary quotation marks (middle of quote) **[5.31]**
13. weekend!"—Punctuation: exclamation mark inside quotes when it applies to material within the quote **[5.24]**

Footnotes in Anatomy Corrected

"Next, we're going to discuss the human foot, which has 26 bones in all," said Mrs. Langdon. "They can be divided into three different kinds." As she pointed at the ankle, Mrs. Langdon said, "Can anyone give the name for the ankle bones?" Becky answered that they were the tarsals. "That's right," Mrs. Langdon said. "The foot has seven tarsal bones. What about the instep bones?" Miguel correctly identified them as the metatarsals. "That's right again," Mrs. Langdon said. "The foot has five metatarsal bones. Who knows what we call the bones in our toes?" Nobody knew, so Mrs. Langdon continued. "The toe bones are called phalanges. The foot has fourteen phalanges. Two are in the big toe, and three are in each of the other four toes. Can anyone guess why the big toe has one fewer bone than the rest of the toes? Oh, there's the bell. We'll have to take up that subject on Monday. Have a great weekend!"

31. Digits Rule in CD

11 errors—2 content; 1 capitalization; 2 grammar; 5 puctuation; 1 usage

Digits Rule in CD Errors

I thought that all I needed was my music[1] but professor[2] Alverson changed my mind. He got my friends and I[3] interested in science. He explained the digital audio technology used in recording and playing back sounds. "A compact disc contains many tiny pits and raised areas [4]"called lands[5]" he said. "It is read by a system that shines a laser beam on the pits and lands as the disc spins by. When the laser beam encounters a pit or a land," he continued, [6]its reflection is changed. The system interprets the change as a 1 or a 0. The CD player uses the information not only to interpret the message,[7] but also to reconstruct it." I'm glad my CD player may[8] translate the analog[9] language into the digital[10] music [11]I and my friends[11] love to hear!

1. *music,* but—Punctuation: comma used before coordinating conjunction joining independent clauses **[5.18, 5.33]**
2. *Professor* Alverson—Capital: title used as part of name **[1.6]**
3. and *me*—Grammar: pronoun as object **[3.19]**
4. *called*—Punctuation: unnecessary quotation marks **[5.31]**
5. *lands,*—Punctuation: comma separates direct quote from speaker **[5.19]**
6. *"its*—Punctuation: quotation marks enclose both parts of a divided quotation **[5.31]**
7. *message* but—Punctuation: comma unnecessary in phrase contrasted through use of correlative conjunctions **[3.11]**
8. *can*—Usage: confused word pair (may/can) **[4.8]**
9. *digital*—Content: see caption **[2.1]**
10. *analog*—Content: see caption **[2.1]**
11. *my friends and I*—Grammar: first person last **[3.19]**

Digits Rule in CD Corrected

I thought that all I needed was my music, but Professor Alverson changed my mind. He got my friends and me interested in science. He explained the digital audio technology used in recording and playing back sounds. "A compact disc contains many tiny pits and raised areas called lands," he said. "It is read by a

system that shines a laser beam on the pits and lands as the disc spins by. When the laser beam encounters a pit or a land," he continued, "its reflection is changed. The system interprets the change as a 1 or a 0. The CD player uses the information not only to interpret the message but also to reconstruct it." I'm glad my CD player can translate the digital language into the analog music my friends and I love to hear!

32. Count on Computers

12 errors—2 content; 8 grammar; 2 punctuation

Count on Computers Errors

We humans like to make things easy for us[1]. Because we have eight fingers and two thumbs, we use the decimal number system. It is based on ten digits. Computers, however, are more suited to the binary, or base two, system. Base two requires only [2]one symbol[2]. A one or a zero can easily [3]in the computer be expressed[3] as either a flow of electricity and[4] no flow of electricity. How do we read an[5] number in base two? On the [6]most far right[6] is the ones place. The next place to the left are[7] the twos place. The third place shows how many fours, the fourth place shows how many eights, and so on. We add all the values that hold ones to get the equivalent decimal number. Therefore, the binary number in the illustration represents our decimal number twenty-two[8]. Since only two states of electric flow need to be used, [9]The binary number system lets computers process information [10]most easiest[10] than they could otherwise. Computers, in turn, can make things easier for ourselves[11]. Awesome[12]

1. *ourselves*—Grammar: reflexive pronoun **[3.20]**
2. *two symbols*—Content: see caption and illustration **[2.1]**
3. *be expressed in the computer*—Usage: misplaced modifier (Acceptable: easily

be expressed as a flow…in the computer.) **[4.6]**

4. *or*—Grammar: correlative conjunctions used in pairs (either/or) **[3.11]**

5. *a* number—Grammar: article *a* used before consonant sound **[3.5]**

6. *farthest* right—Grammar: superlative adjective (Acceptable: rightmost) **[3.9]**

7. *is*—Usage: agreement of verb with subject (place/is) **[4.2]**

8. *twenty-one*—Content: see illustration and caption (add 16, 4, and 1 to get 21) **[2.1]**

9. used, *the*—Punctuation: sentence fragment **[5.38]**

10. *more easily*—Grammar: comparative adverb **[3.9]**

11. *us*—Grammar: pronoun as object (not reflexive) **[3.19, 3.20]**

12. Awesome!—Punctuation: exclamation mark with stand-alone exclamation **[5.23]**

Count on Computers Corrected

We humans like to make things easy for ourselves. Because we have eight fingers and two thumbs, we use the decimal number system. It is based on ten digits. Computers, however, are more suited to the binary, or base two, system. Base two requires only two symbols. A one or a zero can easily be expressed in the computer as either a flow of electricity or no flow of electricity. How do we read a number in base two? On the farthest right is the ones place. The next place to the left is the twos place. The third place shows how many fours, the fourth place shows how many eights, and so on. We add all the values that hold ones to get the equivalent decimal number. Therefore, the binary number in the illustration represents our decimal number twenty-one. Since only two states of electric flow need to be used, the binary number system lets computers process information more easily than they could otherwise.

Computers, in turn, can make things easier for us. Awesome!

33. Animated about Art

15 errors—2 content; 1 capitalization; 6 grammar; 4 punctuation; 2 spelling

Animated about Art Errors

We were excited to hear about jobs at Magic Carpet Studios! We readily lended[1] our ears to supervisor[2] Warren of the animation team. "Layout artists make sketches of all scenes for the animated film. Background artists create tone and style[3] and the animators design the characters. Have you any idea how much research is necessary for the animator's job"?[4] he asked. We told him [5]"that we already knowed[6] of artists whom[7] practically lived with deers[8] to learn their movements. "The animators draw the extreme movements," he continued, [9]but the [10]background artists[10] make all the intermediate drawings. Finally, it is the cleanup artist who draws the [11]more careful[11] of all. This artist must redraw the art and add the final touches. For example," he said as he pointed at a pig's suspenders, "these three[12] buttons must be added at cleanup. It is the cleanup artist who's[13] work will be saw[14] by yourselves[15], the audience."

1. *lent*—Grammar: past tense verb **[3.24]**

2. *Supervisor*—Capital: title used as part of name **[1.6]**

3. *style, and*—Punctuation: comma used before coordinating conjunction joining independent clauses **[5.18, 5.33]**

4. *job?"*—Punctuation: question mark inside quotation marks when it applies to material inside quote **[5.30]**

5. him *that*—Punctuation: unnecessary quotation marks (indirect quote) **[5.31]**

6. *knew*—Grammar: past tense verb **[3.24]**

7. *who*—Grammar: pronoun *who* used as subject **[3.21]**

8. *deer*—Spelling **[6.2]**

9. *"but*—Punctuation: quotation marks enclose both parts of a divided quotation **[5.31]**

10. *inbetweeners*—Content: see caption **[2.1]**

11. *most carefully*—Grammar: superlative adverb **[3.9]**

12. *two*—Content: see illustration **[2.1]**

13. *whose*—Spelling **[6.1]**

14. be *seen*—Grammar: past participle (used in future tense passive voice) **[3.22, 3.24, 3.25]**

15. *you*—Grammar: pronoun as object (not reflexive) **[3.19, 3.20]**

Animated about Art Corrected

We were excited to hear about jobs at Magic Carpet Studios! We readily lent our ears to Supervisor Warren of the animation team. "Layout artists make sketches of all scenes for the animated film. Background artists create tone and style, and the animators design the characters. Have you any idea how much research is necessary for the animator's job?" he asked. We told him that we already knew of artists who practically lived with deer to learn their movements. "The animators draw the extreme movements," he continued, "but the inbetweeners make all the intermediate drawings. Finally, it is the cleanup artist who draws the most carefully of all. This artist must redraw the art and add the final touches. For example," he said as he pointed at a pig's suspenders, "these two buttons must be added at cleanup. It is the cleanup artist whose work will be seen by you, the audience."

GUIDE TO GRAMMAR, USAGE, AND PUNCTUATION

The punctuation, grammar, and usage guidelines that follow cover all the skills used in this book. These skills represent a mid-level English curriculum. This guide is not meant to be a complete English reference. The types of errors are broken down into these areas: capitalization, content, grammar, usage, punctuation, and spelling. Specific topics are listed alphabetically under these main headings.

CAPITALIZATION

1.1 The first word in a sentence is capitalized.

> What a day we had!

1.2 Capitalize the first word in a direct quote. Do not capitalize a sentence fragment or the second half of a divided quotation.

> Jose said, "Come and look at the beautiful new mural on display in the library."
> "Come," Jose said, "and look at the beautiful new mural on display in the library."
> Jose said that he wanted us to see "the beautiful new mural."

1.3 Use a capital letter for a proper noun (not for a general noun). A proper noun names a specific person, place, or thing.

> Paris, France   the World Series   John Doe
> I go to Valley View School.   *but*   I go to the smaller school.

1.4 Use a capital letter for a proper adjective. A proper adjective is derived from a proper noun.

> African tribes   a Southern accent

1.5 Use a capital letter on the abbreviated forms of proper nouns and proper adjectives and initials.

> Nov. 27   U.C.L.A.

1.6 Use a capital letter on people's titles and their abbreviated forms only when they are used as part of a name or in place of a name.

> Captain John Smith   Capt. John Smith   John Smith was the captain.
> Doctor Susan White   Dr. Susan White   We saw the doctor.
> Yes, Captain, the lieutenant has left.   Oh, Doctor, I feel ill!

1.7 Capitalize words of familial relation when used in place of a name.

> At 1:00 Mother called us in for lunch.
> My mother called us in for lunch.

1.8 Capitalize the days of the week, the months, and the holidays. Do not capitalize a season unless it is being personified.

> Monday, December 24   New Year's Day   summer vacation
> as Winter grasped us in its chilly hands

1.9 Capitalize first and last words in the titles of books, songs, articles, poems, and movies. Capitalize all other words except articles, coordinating conjunctions, and prepositions of five or fewer letters (*in, with,* etc.).

> *Gone with the Wind*   *Men in Black*   "God Bless America"

1.10 Capitalize the greeting of a friendly letter.

> Dear Julia,

1.11 Capitalize only the first word in the closing of a friendly letter.

> Sincerely,   Yours truly,   Love

CONTENT 2.1   In the *Editor in Chief*® activities, any discrepancy between the title, illustration, or caption and the accompanying paragraph should be considered an error in the paragraph. Some content errors will be simple differences in information between an illustration/caption and the paragraph. Other content errors will require the student to analyze information from the illustration/caption in order to correct the paragraph.

GRAMMAR   Parts of Speech

Adjectives and Adverbs

Adjectives

3.1   Adjectives modify (give information about) nouns or pronouns. Adjectives tell what kind (*small* house), which one (*this* hat), or how many (*one* child). For more information, see Usage/Agreement on pages 76–7.

3.2   The demonstrative adjectives *this* and *these* are used to indicate something that is nearby, while *that* and *those* are used to indicate something that is farther away.

> Nearby: *this* house, *these* houses
>
> Farther away: *that* house, *those* houses

3.3   Here and there are unnecessary with *this, that, these,* and *those*.

> Incorrect: this here box
>
> Correct: this box

See "Comparing and Contrasting Adjectives and Adverbs" on page 63 for more on using adjectives. See also "Demonstrative Pronouns" on page 67 for more on *this, that, these,* and *those*.

Adverbs

3.4   Adverbs modify verbs, adjectives, or other adverbs. Adverbs tell how, when, where, how often, how much, or to what extent. Regular adverbs are formed by adding *-ly* to an adjective; however, not all words that end in *-ly* are adverbs, and not all adverbs end in *-ly*.

> Example: She ran *quickly*. (quickly modifies verb—tells how she ran)
>
> Example: I swam *yesterday*. (yesterday modifies verb—tells when I swam)
>
> Example: He walked *downtown*. (downtown modifies verb—tells where he walked)
>
> Example: It is *very rarely* hot here. (very modifies adverb; rarely modifies adjective—together they tell how often it is hot)
>
> Example: That is an *extremely* beautiful apple. (extremely modifies adjective—tells to what extent the apple is beautiful)

See "Comparing and Contrasting Adjectives and Adverbs" below for more on using adverbs.

Articles

3.5   Articles (a, an, the) are adjectives. Use *an* before a vowel sound, *a* before a consonant sound. Confusion over which article to use most often comes with words beginning in *h*. If the word clearly begins with a vowel or consonant sound, the standard rule for articles applies. Confusion usually comes with words beginning with *h* in which the *h* is part of an unstressed or lightly stressed first syllable. In such cases, it is considered acceptable to use either *a* or *an*.

> Examples: an hour, a ham
>
> Examples: a historian or an historian, a heroic or an heroic

Comparing and Contrasting Adjectives and Adverbs

3.6   Most (but not all) adverbs end in *-ly*. Adjectives usually don't end in *-ly* (although a few do). Sometimes the same word functions as an adjective and an adverb. Sometimes adverbs of a particular word have more than one form. See the examples below.

Adjective	Adverb	Adverb ending in -ly
a *high* window	He leaped *high*.	We think *highly* of him.
a *close* encounter	He walked *close* to her.	We watched her *closely*.

Adjective ending in -ly	Adverb ending in -ly
nightly train	We go *nightly*.
lively tune	Step *lively*, boys!

These examples show that distinguishing between adverbs and adjectives is not as simple as checking to see whether a word ends in *-ly*. You need to see what the word modifies (describes).

Adjectives modify	Adverbs modify
nouns	verbs
pronouns	adjectives
	other adverbs

> Adjective: It rained *last* night. (*last* tells which night; it modifies the noun night)
>
> Adverb: Our team played *last*. (*last* tells when the team played; it modifies the verb played)

3.7   Linking verbs are frequently followed by adjectives.

> Adjective: She looked *pretty*. (*pretty* modifies the subject she)
>
> Adjective: He sounded *happy*. (*happy* modifies the subject he)
>
> Adjective: He felt *bad*. (*bad* modifies the subject he)

Many verbs that function as linking verbs can also be used as action verbs. In these cases, the action verbs will be followed by adverbs rather than adjectives.

> Linking verb with adjective: He stayed *quiet*. (*quiet* modifies the subject he)
>
> Action verb with adverb: He stayed *quietly* in his seat. (*quietly* modifies the verb stayed; it tells how he stayed in his seat)

Linking verbs take adjectives. Action verbs take adverbs. See "Linking Verbs" on page 72.

Well/Good

3.8   As modifiers, *well* and *good* are sometimes a source of confusion. *Well* is both an adverb and an adjective; *good* is only an adjective.

Perhaps some of the confusion comes because well and good occasionally overlap in meaning. You can say either "He feels well" or "He feels good" to indicate a general state of health. *Good* is not just limited to describing health, however. You can say "He feels good about his promotion." *Well* cannot be used in this way. As an adjective, *well* has only three meanings:

1. to be healthy
   He looks *well*.
2. to look well-dressed or well-groomed
   He looks *well* in a suit.
3. to be satisfactory, right, or proper
   It is *well* to fulfill your commitments.

Good, on the other hand, is always an adjective. It cannot be used to modify a verb. In the examples below, *well* and *good* convey similar meanings, but they do so by modifying different types of words.

Good: You did a *good* job. (*good* is an adjective; it modifies job)

Well: You did *well*. (*well* is an adverb; it modifies did)

Another source of confusion may be that the comparative and superlative forms are the same for *good* and *well*: good, better, best and well, better, best. See below.

Comparative and Superlative Forms of Adjectives and Adverbs

3.9   Comparative and superlative forms of adjectives and adverbs are used to compare the degrees of characteristics possessed by the objects that they modify.

Most one-syllable adjectives/adverbs add the suffix *-er* or *-est*.

hot—hotter—hottest   small—smaller—smallest
lucky—luckier—luckiest

Some adjectives/adverbs use more/most to create the comparative and superlative forms.

quietly—more quietly—most quietly
beautiful—more beautiful—most beautiful

Less and least can also be used to create comparative and superlative forms.

aggressive—less aggressive—least aggressive
powerful—less powerful—least powerful

Irregular comparative forms

good/well—better—best

bad—worse—worst

many/much—more—most

Whether you use the comparative or superlative form (rather than the simple positive form) depends on how many things are being compared.

Comparative: The comparative form of adjectives and adverbs is used when comparing two items, two groups, or one item with a group.

He is the *older* of two children. (adjective)

The Jets are *better* than the Eagles. (adjective)

She runs *faster* than the boys. (adverb) *Note that she is not part of the boys.*

Superlative: The superlative form is used when comparing more than two things.

He is the *oldest* child of seven. (adjective)

The Jets are the sharpest of all the teams. (adjective)

She is the best player on the team. (adjective) *Note that she is part of the team.*

He sings the most beautifully. (adverb)

Conjunctions

The word *conjunction* refers to joining or coming together. We use conjunctions to join various grammatical elements: words, phrases, clauses. There are three kinds of conjunctions: coordinating, correlative, and subordinating. Each of these three types of conjunctions is described below.

Coordinating Conjunctions

3.10   Coordinating conjunctions join words, phrases, clauses, or sentences. The word *coordinating* indicates that the elements that are joined have equal grammatical weight—for example, nouns with other nouns, verbs with other verbs, clauses with other clauses of equal rank. Another way to think of this is that coordinating conjunctions join constructions that are parallel.

He *ran and jumped*. (verb with verb)

We could use a new *car or truck*. (noun with noun)

I saw *two of my friends but none of my relatives* at the wedding. (2 phrases)

She had a new computer, so she took a class on home computing. (2 independent clauses)

There are seven coordinating conjunctions. To assist in remembering these conjunctions, use their first letters to form a mnemonic aid: FAN BOYS—**f**or, **a**nd, **n**or, **b**ut, **o**r, **y**et, **s**o.

When a coordinating conjunction joins two independent clauses, or main clauses, it should be preceded by a comma unless the independent clauses are short and closely related.

He came and he went.

We went to Paris, but we stayed only a few days.

Correlative Conjunctions

3.11   Correlative conjunctions is the name given to coordinating conjunctions used in pairs. The following are common correlative conjunctions:

either...or   neither...nor   both...and   not only...but (also)
whether...or

As with the other coordinating conjunctions, correlative conjunctions join elements of similar grammatical construction, e.g., two adjectives, two prepositional phrases, two independent clauses, etc. Correlative conjunctions should be placed as close as possible to the elements they join.

>Misplaced: Either *we will go to the lake* or *to the seashore.* (joins independent clause and prepositional phrase)

>Correct: We will go either *to the lake* or *to the seashore.* (joins 2 prepositional phrases)

In general, correlative conjunctions do not require commas; however, they may need a comma if they join two independent clauses. In the first example below, *not only...but* joins two independent clauses. In the second example, the same correlative conjunction joins two nouns (*cat* and *dog*).

>Not only do we have to wash the car, but we also must shampoo the carpets.

>We have not only a cat but also a dog.

Subordinating Conjunctions

3.12 Subordinating conjunctions join subordinate, or dependent, clauses to independent clauses. The following are commonly used subordinating conjunctions:

after	even though	than	wherever
although	how	that	whether
as	if	though	while
as if	in order that	unless	
as though	inasmuch as	until	
as much as	provided	when	
because	since	whenever	
before	so that	where	

Anytime a subordinating conjunction begins a clause, that clause will be a subordinate clause. This is true even if the clause that follows the conjunction would otherwise be an independent clause.

>Independent clause: *we left the party*

>Subordinate clause: *after we left the party*

3.13 In general, when a sentence consists of a dependent clause followed by an independent clause, the dependent clause should be followed by a comma.

>Dependent clause + independent clause: After we left the party, we went for a walk.

>Dependent clause + independent clause: While the neighbors were away, the dog dug up the roses.

3.14 In general, when a dependent clause beginning with a subordinating conjunction follows an independent clause, no comma is required.

>Independent clause + dependent clause: We went for a walk after we left the party.

>Independent clause + dependent clause: The dog dug up the roses while the neighbors were away.

Beginning writers often insert commas before clauses beginning with the conjunctions *since* and *because.* *Since* and *because,* however, are subordinating, not coordinating, conjunctions. This means that even if *since* or *because* is followed by an independent clause, that clause is made subordinate by *since* or *because*. Such sentences containing *since* or *because* are examples of independent clauses + dependent clauses and do not require a comma.

> Example: We went right home from the store because we were afraid the ice cream would melt.

> Example: I wanted to ask him about the football game since I knew he had seen it.

For more on independent and dependent clauses, see "Clauses" on page 73 and "Clauses and Punctuation" on page 82.

Pronouns

Demonstrative Pronouns

3.15   When used alone (not modifying a noun), *this*, *that*, *these*, and *those* function as nouns and are considered demonstrative pronouns.

> *This* is a very nice rug.

> *Those* are pretty flowers.

In addition to identifying people or things, the demonstrative pronouns can be used to indicate spatial relationships.

> *This* is my house; *that* is my sister's. (This one is nearby; that one is farther away.)

Indefinite Pronouns

3.16   An indefinite pronoun does not refer to a specific person or thing. Some common indefinite pronouns are listed below.

all	everybody	no one
another	everyone	one
any	everything	other
anybody	few	several
anyone	many	some
anything	much	somebody
both	most	someone
each	neither	something
each one	nobody	such
either	none	

Indefinite pronouns are often used to make general statements or to indicate quantity.

> *Everybody* knows how upset she was.

> *Most* of the band members showed up for practice.

3.17   Unlike personal pronouns, indefinite pronouns use an apostrophe and *s* to form the possessive.

> *Everyone's* cars got muddy after the storm.

> He felt that *one's* actions should reflect *one's* beliefs.

3.18   Note that if the indefinite pronoun is used as a possessive with *else*,

else takes the apostrophe and *s*.

> *No one else's* project looked as good as hers.

Personal Pronouns

3.19   A personal pronoun replaces a noun or nouns. The pronoun must always agree in number and gender with the noun or nouns it replaces (see Agreement: Pronoun with Antecedent, pages 74–5). Pronouns may be used as subjects or objects in a sentence.

> Subject: *We* children are hungry.
>
> Object: Give some food to *us* children.

When a pronoun is used as the subject in a sentence, the verb must agree with the pronoun in number (see Agreement: Verb with Subject, page 75).

Pronouns may also show possession. A possessive pronoun may be used before a noun to show possession (*my* bike), or a possessive pronoun may stand alone. (The bike is *mine*.) Note that unlike most nouns, possessive pronouns do not use an apostrophe to form the possessive.

Singular/ Plural	Person	Subject	Object	Possessive before noun	Possessive stands alone
singular	first person	I	me	my	mine
singular	second person	you	you	your	yours
singular	third person	he	him	his	his
singular	third person	she	her	her	hers
singular	third person	it	it	its	its
plural	first person	we	us	our	ours
plural	second person	you	you	your	yours
plural	third person	they	them	their	theirs

Confusion in pronoun usage frequently occurs with compound subjects or objects (Marla and I, him and me). The easiest way to determine the correct form of the pronoun is to look at each member of the compound subject or object separately, as in these examples:

> Marla and I went home. (*Marla* went home. *I* went home.)
>
> Kim Lee went with him and me. (Kim Lee went with *him*. Kim Lee went with *me*.)
>
> Bruce and he saw the movie. (*Bruce* saw the movie. *He* saw the movie.)

When the compound subject is broken apart in this way, most native speakers will recognize the correct pronoun form.

Note that the first person pronouns (I, me/we, us) always appear last in compound subjects and objects.

Reflexive and Intensive Pronouns

3.20   Reflexive and intensive pronouns use the same form. They are pronouns that end in *-self* or *-selves*: myself, yourself, herself, himself, itself, ourselves, yourselves, and themselves. They are used to refer to (reflexive) or emphasize (intensive) another noun or pronoun within the sentence.

Reflexive: A reflexive pronoun "reflects" back on an antecedent (the noun or pronoun to which it refers) that is within the same sentence.

Reflexive: I went by *myself*. (antecedent = I)

Reflexive: We could have done that *ourselves*. (antecedent = we)

Intensive: An intensive pronoun is used to emphasize or intensify an antecedent that is next to it within the same sentence.

Intensive: The girls *themselves* thought of the idea. (antecedent = the girls)

Intensive: You *yourself* may have seen something similar. (antecedent = you)

Subject	Object	Possessive
who	whom	whose
whoever	whomever	whosever

Note that both reflexive and intensive pronouns must have an antecedent that is within the same sentence. There is sometimes a tendency to use these pronouns incorrectly in place of personal pronouns.

Incorrect: She and *myself* went to the store after school. (no antecedent for *myself* in this sentence)

Correct: She and *I* went to the store after school.

Incorrect: He went with *myself*. (no antecedent for *myself* in this sentence)

Correct: He went with *me*.

Who and Whom

3.21   Who and whoever have three different forms depending upon their function in the sentence: subject, object, possessive.

There is often a great deal of confusion over whether to use *who* or *whom*. If it functions as the subject, use who; if it functions as the object, use whom. The difficulty often lies in deciding whether you need a subject or object.

Subject: Who is coming for dinner?

Object: Whom are we waiting for?

The easiest way to decide whether to use who or whom (or whoever or whomever) is to mentally drop who/whom and the words preceding it and make a sentence with the words that are left by adding he or him. If you would use *he*, then the sentence needs a subject, and you should use *who*. If you would use *him*, then the sentence needs an object, and you should use *whom*. See the examples below.

Sentence: Do you know who/whom will be attending the meeting?

Remove who/whom: *will be attending the meeting*

Add he or him: *He* will be attending the meeting.

Correct: Do you know *who* will be attending the meeting?

Sentence: Who/whom is the party for?

Remove who/whom: *is the party for*

Add he or him: Is the party for *him*?

Correct: *Whom* is the party for?

Verbs

Verb Parts

3.22   All verbs have four principal parts: infinitive (sometimes called "plain verb"), present participle, past, and past participle. Present and past participles are used with helping verbs to form verb phrases. Regular verbs form the past and past participle by adding -*d* or -*ed* to the infinitive. Irregular verbs form the past and past participle forms in a different way, such as by changing spelling or by not changing at all.

Regular Verbs

Infinitive	Present Participle	Past	Past Participle
care	caring	cared	cared
call	calling	called	called
jump	jumping	jumped	jumped
walk	walking	walked	walked

Irregular Verbs

Infinitive	Present Participle	Past	Past Participle
bring	bringing	brought	brought
choose	choosing	chose	chosen
go	going	went	gone
ride	riding	rode	ridden
think	thinking	thought	thought
pay	paying	paid	paid
know	knowing	know	known
shrink	shrinking	shrank (or shrunk)	shrunk (or shrunken)

Verb Phrase

3.23   A verb phrase consists of a main verb and one or more helping verbs (also called auxiliary verbs). A few verb phrases are listed below:

has gone   is going   will have gone   will be going

Since many verb phrases are formed using the verb *to be*, we review its parts below:

Infinitive	Present Participle	Past	Past Participle
be	being	was, were	been

Verb Tense

3.24   Tense refers to the time element expressed by a verb. Verb tense shows whether an action has already occurred, is now occurring, or will occur in the future. Although there are four principal parts to verbs, these four parts are used to form six tenses: present tense, past tense, future tense, present perfect tense, past perfect tense, future perfect tense. These tenses can be subdivided into progressive form (be + present participle). Present and past can be further subdivided into emphatic.

Tense	Part of Verb Used	Example
present tense	Active: infinitive (Passive: be + past participle)	Active: I ask. (Passive: I am asked.)
present progressive	be + present participle	I am asking.
present emphatic	do + infinitive	I do ask.
present perfect tense	have or has + past participle	I have asked.
present perfect progressive	have or has + be (past participle) + present participle	I have been asking.
past tense	Active: past (Passive: be [past] and past participle)	Active: I asked. (Passive: I was asked.)
past progressive	be (past) + present participle	I was asking.
past emphatic	do (past) + infinitive	I did ask.
past perfect tense	had + past participle	I had asked.
past perfect progressive	had + be (past participle) + present participle	I had been asking.
future tense	Active: will or shall + infinitive (Passive: will or shall + be + past participle)	Active: I will ask. (Passive: I will be asked.)
future progressive	will or shall + be (infinitive) + present participle	I will be asking.
future perfect tense	will (or shall) have + past participle	I will have asked.
future perfect progressive	will (or shall) have + be (past participle) + present participle	I will have been asking.

Irregular verb forms are sometimes confused. For example, in the verb *do*, the simple past tense *did* is sometimes incorrectly substituted for the past participle *done* in the perfect tenses. This results in *have did* (wrong) for *have done* (right). The past participles of both *do* and *go* are always used with a helping verb to create the present perfect, the past perfect, and the future perfect tenses.

Simple Past	Perfect tenses used with *past participle*		
did	have *done* (not *did)*	had *done*	will have *done*
went	have *gone* (not *went)*	had *gone*	will have *gone*

Participles

3.25 The present participle is used with a form of the verb *be* in the progressive tense. The form of *be* determines whether the sentence is present or past progressive.

Progressive = *be* + present participle

> Present progressive: The boy is flying a kite.

> Past progressive: The boy was flying a kite.

The past participle is used with a form of the verb *be* in passive voice. In passive voice, the subject of the sentence is being acted upon rather than acting.

Passive voice = *be* + past participle

> Passive voice (present): A kite is flown by the boy.

> Passive voice (past): A kite was flown by the boy.

Below are examples of active and passive voice in various tenses.

Active (present): The dog chases the birds.

Active (present perfect): The dog has chased the birds.

Active (past): The dog chased the birds.

Active (past perfect): The dog had chased the birds.

Active (future): The dog will chase the birds.

Active (future perfect): The dog will have chased the birds.

Active (present progressive): The dog is chasing the birds.

Active (present perfect progressive): The dog has been chasing the birds.

Active (past progressive): The dog was chasing the birds.

Active (past perfect progressive): The dog had been chasing the birds.

Active (future progressive): The dog will be chasing the birds.

Active (future perfect progressive): The dog will have been chasing the birds.

Passive (present): The birds are chased by the dog.

Passive (present perfect): The birds have been chased by the dog.

Passive (past): The birds were chased by the dog.

Passive (past perfect): The birds had been chased by the dog.

Passive (future): The birds will be chased by the dog.

Passive (future perfect): The birds will have been chased by the dog.

Passive (present progressive): The birds are being chased by the dog.

Passive (past progressive): The birds were being chased by the dog.

Helping Verbs

3.26   A helping verb (also called an auxiliary verb) is part of a verb phrase. A verb phrase consists of a main verb and a helping verb. Future tense, perfect tense, progressive form, and passive voice are all created using helping verbs.

Below are verb phrases with the helping verb marked in italics:

has written	*may* attend	*can* ski	*might have* seen
must read	*will* ride	*shall* go	*would have* taken

Common helping verbs include the following: be, can, could, do, have, may, might, must, shall, should, will, would.

Linking Verbs

3.27   Linking verbs express a state or condition rather than an action. They are called linking verbs because they link the subject to a complement which identifies or describes the subject. This subject complement may be a noun, pronoun, or adjective. Common linking verbs include the following: appear, be, become, feel, grow, look, remain, seem, smell, sound, stay, taste.

Anchovies *taste* salty.

That dog *looks* thin.

She *is* the manager.

Some linking verbs can also be used as action verbs, which can be modified by adverbs. A good way to determine whether the verb is functioning as a linking verb or action verb is to substitute the appropriate forms of *is* and *seem* for the verb. If the sentence still makes sense and has not changed its meaning, then the verb is a linking verb.

> Linking verb: He remains happy. (No meaning change—He *is* happy. He *seems* happy.)
>
> Action verb: He remains happily at the park. (Meaning changes—He *is* happily at the park. He *seems* happily at the park.)

Linking verbs take adjectives. Action verbs take adverbs.

Usage note: *Seem* is always a linking verb. When used as the main verb, *be* is a linking verb except when followed by an adverb. See "Comparing and Contrasting Adjectives and Adverbs" on page 63.

Parts of a Sentence

Clauses

All clauses contain a subject and a predicate. The fact that clauses have both a subject and a predicate distinguishes them from phrases (see "Phrases" below). Phrases may contain a subject or verb but not both.

Clauses are classified as to whether or not they make sense standing alone. Clauses fall into two main categories: (1) clauses that make sense standing alone are called independent, or main, clauses and (2) clauses that do not make sense standing alone are called dependent, or subordinate, clauses.

Independent Clause/Main Clause

3.28   The terms *independent clause* and *main clause* can be used interchangeably. Independent, or main, clauses make sense standing alone. Adding an initial capital and ending punctuation transforms an independent clause into a simple sentence. Many sentences consist of nothing but an independent clause; however, a sentence may also contain one or more dependent clauses and even additional independent clauses.

> Independent clause: it was a hot, humid day
>
> Independent clause: I needed a cool drink
>
> Two simple sentences: It was a hot, humid day. I needed a cool drink.

Note that by definition an independent clause is not a sentence. The terms *independent,* or *main, clause* and *sentence* refer to different levels of grammatical construction and cannot be used interchangeably. An independent clause is a group of words that represent a complete thought and contain a subject and verb. In addition, a sentence must begin with a capital letter and end with an appropriate punctuation mark.

Dependent Clause/Subordinate Clause

3.29   The terms *dependent clause* and *subordinate clause* can be used interchangeably. A subordinate, or dependent, clause does not represent a complete thought and cannot stand alone.

Dependent clause: *where my brother had gone*

Dependent clause: *whom he was seeing*

Dependent clauses must be combined with independent clauses in order to form sentences. In the sentences below, *we knew* and *we wondered* are independent clauses.

Simple sentence: We knew *where my brother had gone.*

Simple sentence: We wondered *whom he was seeing.*

For information on punctuating sentences containing independent and dependent clauses, see "Clauses and Punctuation" page 82.

Phrases

3.30   In casual conversation, *phrase* refers to any group of words that function together. In the study of English, however, *phrase* has a more specific meaning, and we distinguish between phrases and clauses (see "Clauses" above). All groups of words that function together are either clauses (which contain both a subject and a verb) or nonclauses (which do not contain both a subject and a verb); nonclauses are phrases. So a phrase is a group of words that act as a unit and contain either a subject or a verb but not both.

Phrases may function as nouns, verbs, or modifiers. Phrases may be located anywhere in a sentence, but when they begin a sentence, they are usually followed by a comma. Phrases must always be part of a sentence. Like dependent clauses, phrases cannot stand alone. If a phrase is not part of a complete sentence, it is a sentence fragment.

Walking to the park was fun. (phrase functioning as a noun)

The dog *was running* quickly. (phrase functioning as a verb)

That is the prettiest flower *in the garden*. (phrase functioning as an adjective—modifies flower)

We went *to the mall*. (phrase functioning as an adverb—modifies went)

Phrases tend be confused with dependent clauses because neither of them forms a complete thought. Remember, a clause will have both a subject and a verb, and a phrase will have one or the other but not both.

Subject

3.31   Subject: Use a noun or pronoun (not both) as subject.

Incorrect: Marnie she had a lovely coat.

Correct: Marnie had a lovely coat.

Correct: She had a lovely coat.

USAGE

Agreement

Agreement: Pronoun with Antecedent

4.1   A pronoun must agree with its antecedent in number, gender, and person. The antecedent is the noun or noun phrase to which the pronoun refers.

> Sentence: *The kittens* chased the mouse. (replace *the kittens* with a pronoun)
>
> Plural antecedent—plural pronoun: *They* chased the mouse.
>
> Sentence: *The boy* flew a kite. (replace *the boy* with a pronoun)
>
> Singular, masculine antecedent—singular, masculine pronoun: *He* flew a kite.

Agreement: Verb with Subject

4.2   A subject and verb agree if they are both singular or both plural, that is, the subject and verb must agree in number.

Nouns are singular when they refer to one person, place, or thing and plural when they refer to more than one (cat—singular, cats—plural).

Most verbs ending in *s* are singular, while verbs not ending in *s* are plural. The exception to this general rule is verbs used with *I* and singular *you* (which take the same verb form as plural *you).* Although *I* and *you* are singular, their verbs do not take an *s*: I go, you go, he goes, it goes, they go, we go.

The number of the subject is not affected by any phrases that fall between the subject and the verb. (See "Agreement: Verb with Indefinite Pronouns" on page 76 for the only exception.)

> Sentence: The difficulties of going on a long trip were apparent.
>
> Subject: the difficulties (plural)
>
> Verb: were (plural)

The verb should agree with the subject even when the subject and predicate are inverted.

> Performing for the first time on this stage are the Lowell sisters. (subject = Lowell sisters, plural verb = are)
>
> Performing for the first time on this stage is Winifred Lowell. (subject = Winifred Lowell, singular verb = is)

Agreement: Verb with Compound Subject

4.3   Compound subjects are formed by joining words or groups of words with *and, or,* or *nor*.

Subjects joined with *and* take a plural verb. This is true whether the words making up the compound subject are singular or plural.

> Single subject: Our cat spends a lot of time in the back yard.
>
> Compound subject: Our cat and dog spend a lot of time in the back yard.
>
> Compound subject: Our cats and dogs spend a lot of time in the back yard.
>
> Compound subject: Our cat and dogs spend a lot of time in the back yard.
>
> Compound subject: Our cats and dog spend a lot of time in the back yard.

Note that sometimes *and* is used as part of a phrase that functions as a unit to name a single item. In these cases, the subject is not a compound subject.

> Example: Macaroni and cheese is my favorite dish.
>
> Example: Stop and Go was the name of the market.

Singular subjects joined with *or* or *nor* take a singular verb.

Example: A chair or a stool fits under the counter.

Example: Either our cat or our dog sits on the couch.

Example: Neither Melissa nor Jody plays the clarinet.

When plural subjects are joined with *or* or *nor*, they take a plural verb.

Example: Jackets or sweaters are needed in the evenings.

Example: Either his parents or my parents take us to the pool.

Example: Neither our cats nor our dogs like to have baths.

When a plural subject and a singular subject are joined with *or* or *nor*, make the verb agree with the closer of the two subjects.

Example: A sports coat or evening clothes are required for the dinner party.

Example: Evening clothes or a sports coat is required for the dinner party.

Example: Either my parents or my aunt drives us to school.

Example: Either my aunt or my parents drive us to school.

Example: Neither the secretaries nor the supervisor was happy about the arrangement.

Example: Neither the supervisor nor the secretaries were happy about the arrangement.

Agreement: Verb with Indefinite Pronoun

4.4   The verb must agree with the indefinite pronoun in number. Some of the indefinite pronouns take singular verbs, others take plural verbs, and others vary depending on context.

Singular: another, anybody, anyone, anything, each, each one, either, everybody, everyone, everything, much, neither, nobody, no one, one, other, somebody, someone, something

Everybody has a car.   Each of the parents has a car.

Plural: both, few, many, several

Both students have cars.   Several students have cars.

Vary (sometimes singular, sometimes plural): all, any, most, none, some

Most of the cars were dirty.   Most of the car was dirty.

Note that the indefinite pronouns that can be either singular or plural *(all, any, most, none, some)* constitute an exception to the standard rule of agreement that the number of the subject is not affected by any phrases that fall between the subject and the verb. When *all, any, most, none,* or *some* refer to a singular noun, they take a singular verb. When they refer to a plural noun, they take a plural verb.

Singular: *Some* of the paper *is* dry.

Plural: *Some* of the papers *are* on the desk.

Agreement: Adjective with Noun/Pronoun

4.5   An adjective and the noun or pronoun it modifies must agree in number.

She has *two* brothers.

When *this, that, these,* and *those* are used as adjectives, they must agree in number with the noun or pronoun that they are modifying.

> Singular: *this* bird, *that* alligator
>
> Plural: *these* sparrows, *those* crocodiles

Misplaced Modifier

4.6   Modifiers describe, define, clarify, or provide more explicit information about the words they modify. There is nothing intrinsic to the modifiers themselves that shows which word they modify; therefore, modifiers must be carefully placed in sentences so that it is clear which words they modify. Modifiers are said to be misplaced when it is unclear which word they modify or when they modify the wrong word. In general, modifiers should be placed as close as possible to the words they modify. Frequently, misplaced modifiers can be corrected simply by moving the ambiguous phrase closer to the word it modifies.

> Misplaced: I spoke with the woman who is standing by the potted palm in the yellow dress.

In the example above, the reader may think that the palm is draped in a yellow dress. Correct this confusion by relocating the modifier.

> Corrected: I spoke with the woman in the yellow dress who is standing by the potted palm.

Now there is no confusion over who is wearing the yellow dress. In the example below, there is some confusion over who is in the back of the truck.

> Misplaced: He took the dog when he left this morning in the back of the truck.
>
> Correction 1: When he left this morning, he took the dog in the back of the truck.

Now it is clear who is in the back of the truck. There may still be confusion as to whether he took the dog who was already in the back of the truck out of the truck, or he drove the truck as the dog rode in the back.

> Correction 2: When he drove away in the truck this morning, the dog rode in the back.

Now it should be clear that the dog rode.

Unnecessary Words

4.7   Unnecessary words should be deleted.

Negatives: Use only one negative word to state a negative idea.

> Incorrect: We don't have no bananas.
>
> Correct: We don't have any bananas.
>
> Correct: We have no bananas.

The words hardly and scarcely are also considered negative words and should not be used with other negatives.

Incorrect: We have hardly no bananas.

Correct: We have hardly any bananas.

Correct: We have no bananas.

Some words are excessive or repetitive and should be deleted. (See also Subject on page 74.)

Incorrect: The thing is is the people are hungry.

Correct: The people are hungry. (or The thing is, the people are hungry.)

Incorrect: Rover he ran away.

Correct: Rover ran away. (or He ran away.)

Special (Confused) Word Pairs

4.8   There are a number of word pairs that are often confused (effect/affect, continually/continuously). In this level of *Editor in Chief*®, we focus on the following frequently confused pairs of words:

bring (to carry something with oneself to a place—from there to here—when you bring something with you, you arrive with it) / take (to carry to another place—from here to there—when you take something with you, you leave with it)

lay (to put or place) / lie (to rest or recline)

leave (to go away) / let (to allow)

may (to be permitted to) / can (to be able to)

raise (to move something to a higher position, to elevate—transitive verb—you raise objects) / rise (to move from lower to higher—intransitive verb—people/objects rise on their own)

teach (to instruct) / learn (to gain knowledge or understanding)

Note: Some words are used incorrectly because of confusion in construction of irregular verb tenses (e.g., I have <u>went</u> instead of I have <u>gone</u> or I <u>went</u>, etc.) See Verb Tenses on pages 70–1.

PUNCTUATION

Apostrophe

5.1   Use an apostrophe in contractions to show where letters or numbers have been left out.

could not = couldn't   let us = let's   it is = it's

the 1990s = the '90s

5.2   Use an apostrophe to form the plural of letters, but do not use an apostrophe to form the plural of numbers.

Mind your p's and q's.

Shakespeare lived in the late 1500s and early 1600s.

Usage note: At one time, forming the plural of numbers by adding apostrophe *s* was common; however, in current style manuals, the preference is to drop the apostrophe. If you wish to use an apostrophe when forming plural numbers, note that under no circumstances is the construction '90's considered correct.

5.3   Use an apostrophe to form the possessive.

Add *'s* to form the singular possessive.

> dog's bone   Maria's ball   car's color

Add an apostrophe to form the possessive of a plural ending in *-s*, *-es*, or *-ies*.

> cats' toys   foxes' holes   butterflies' flowers

Add *'s* to form the possessive of plural nouns that do not end in *s*.

> women's hats   sheep's wool   children's toys

Usage notes: Pronouns do not use an apostrophe to form the possessive (see "Personal Pronouns" on page 68).
Apostrophes are unnecessary with the regular plurals of words (*the parents of the boys*).

Colon

5.4   Use a colon between numbers indicating hours and minutes.

> We will arrive at 9:15.

5.5   A colon follows the greeting in a business letter.

> Dear Sir: Dear Dr. Martinez:

Comma

5.6   Use a comma between words or phrases in a series

> blue, red, and green   up the hill, over the log, and down the hole

Usage note: At one time, including a comma before the *and* in a series was considered optional. This trend has changed. Including the comma is now the preferred pattern of punctuation.

5.7   Use a comma to separate the elements of an address (street and city, city and state). Note: do not use a comma between the state and ZIP code.

> 5 Elm Street, Sample Town, New York 13635

5.8   Use a comma after the state in a sentence when using the format city, state.

> We are going to Sample Town, New York, to visit our grandmother.

5.9   Use a comma in dates between day and year in the format *month day, year*.

> January 10, 1996   April 5, 2001

Usage note: If you follow the European model, write 9 May 1999— no commas.

5.10   Use a comma after the year in a sentence when using the format *month day, year*.

> We have to be in Nevada on January 10, 1996, in order to visit our friends.

5.11   Use a comma after the greeting of a friendly letter.

> Dear Emilio,

Usage note: Business letters use a colon after the salutation. (See 5.5 above.)

5.12 Use a comma after the closing of a letter (business or friendly).

Sincerely,   With best wishes,   Love,

5.13 Use commas to separate nouns of address from the rest of the sentence.

Kim, I asked you to step over here.

You know, Rebecca, we could go to the store tomorrow.

5.14 Use a comma to separate an introductory word or interjection from the rest of the sentence.

Yes, I have heard of that TV show.   Hey, did you see that comet?

Well, I guess that's true.

5.15 Use a comma to set off an introductory phrase or dependent clause.

After we left, she phoned the office.

From the couch, the cat jumped onto the bookcase.

Usage note: Dependent clauses are also referred to as subordinate clauses. See "Subordinating Conjunctions" page 66 for more information.

5.16 Set off a nonessential (nonrestrictive) appositive with commas. (An appositive is a noun or noun/pronoun phrase, next to a noun, that identifies, defines, or explains the noun.) See "Clauses and Punctuation" pages 82–3 for more on essential/nonessential.

The Marsdens, our nearest neighbors, left on vacation today.

My brother's dog, the big white one, is rolling in the leaves.

5.17 Use commas to set off sentence interrupters.

The recent game, on the other hand, showed the wisdom of working on set plays.

He had told us, however, that he would study more.

5.18 Use commas before coordinating conjunctions joining two independent clauses.

We took the bus, but she will take the train.

My sister mowed the lawn, and I raked the leaves.

He ran outside and shouted to his sister.

Usage note: See "Conjunctions" on page 65 for more information.

5.19 Use a comma to separate a direct quote from a phrase identifying the speaker.

Tomas said, "We had fun doing English today."

"We had fun doing English today," Tomas said.

5.20 Place commas inside ending quotation marks.

The package was marked "fragile," but the contents were quite sturdy.

"We had fun doing English today," Tomas said.

Usage note: We have noted some confusion over this particular rule, possibly because British usage differs from American usage. American style manuals, however, are all in agreement: commas and periods always go inside closing quotation marks.

5.21 Commas are sometimes used inappropriately. Below are some of the more common errors in comma usage. No comma should be used

between a subject and its verb:

Incorrect: The chairman of the arts, told the committee to vote.

with a compound predicate:

Incorrect: The barking dog chased the mailman, and bit him.

with an essential clause:

Incorrect: The manager quit, because she was planning to move.

Incorrect: He mowed the yard, in exchange for a meal.

Exclamation Point

5.22 Use an exclamation point after an exclamatory sentence.

Stop that dog!   We know what to do!   I love chocolate!

5.23 Use an exclamation point after an interjection that stands alone.

Stop! Don't you know to look both ways before crossing a street?

Usage note: An interjection that begins a sentence may function as an introductory word and be set off from the sentence with a comma instead of an exclamation point; for example, Hey, wait for me!

5.24 Place the exclamation point inside quotation marks at the end of a quoted exclamation. (Place it outside when the exclamation applies to the entire sentence.)

Incorrect: "Get that snake off the counter"! screamed Jamie.

Correct: "Get that snake off the counter!" screamed Jamie.

Incorrect: I love my talking "dog!"

Correct: I love my talking "dog"!

Usage note: In contrast to commas and periods (which always fall inside closing quotation marks), an exclamation point falls inside closing quotation marks only when it applies to what is inside the quotation marks. If it is not part of the quoted material, it goes outside the quotation marks; for example, That box is marked "fragile"!

Hyphen

5.25 Use a hyphen with compound numbers.

twenty-five   ninety-four   forty-three

Period

5.26 Use a period to end a declarative sentence.

A sentence begins with a capital letter and ends with a punctuation mark.

5.27 Use a period after abbreviations and initials.

Washington, D.C.   Dr. Nolan   Mr. J. Pedrewski

Note: It is becoming more acceptable to use some common abbreviations without periods, e.g., mph, km, etc. However, for the purposes of consistency in this series, use the periods with abbreviations.

5.28 Always place periods inside closing quotation marks.

We delivered a package marked "fragile."

See usage note under *comma*.

Question Mark

5.29 Use a question mark after a direct question (interrogative sentence).

Are we there yet?   What time is it?

5.30 Place a question mark inside the quotation marks after a quoted question but outside the quotation marks when it doesn't apply to the material in quotation marks.

"What day is soccer practice?" asked Lucia.

Did you see "The End of Earth"?

Usage note: Again in contrast to commas and periods (which always fall inside closing quotation marks), a question mark falls inside closing quotation marks only when it applies to what is inside the quotation marks. In the following, the question mark applies to the entire sentence, not the word inside the quotation marks: Is that box marked "fragile"?

Quotation Marks

5.31 Use quotation marks to enclose direct quotes; enclose both parts of a divided quotation. (Do not use quotation marks with indirect quotes.)

"I need help on this English paper," said Grover.

"This beautiful day," said Mark, "is too good to waste indoors."

He said that it was a beautiful day.

5.32 Quotation marks are used to identify the title of a song, story, poem, article, or book chapter.

We have to memorize "Jabberwocky" by Thursday.

Clauses and Punctuation

Recognizing dependent and independent clauses is useful when punctuating sentences. In some instances, commas are required between dependent and independent clauses, and in other cases, they are not. Following are a few simple rules of thumb for when to use commas in sentences containing clauses:

5.33 independent clause + independent clause =

comma after the first clause when the clauses are joined by a coordinating conjunction

Example: The sun was shining brightly, and the weather was warm.

5.34   independent clause + independent clause =

semicolon after the first clause when the clauses are not joined by a coordinating conjunction

Example: The sun was shining brightly; the weather was warm.

5.35   dependent clause + independent clause =

comma after the dependent clause

Example: After we left for the country, the package we were waiting for arrived.

5.36   independent clause + dependent clause =

varies depending on whether the dependent clause is essential (restrictive) or nonessential (nonrestrictive)

Essential (restrictive) clauses are essential to the meaning of the sentence. Removing them would change the meaning of the sentence. Nonessential (nonrestrictive) clauses can be removed without altering the meaning of the sentence. Nonessential clauses give additional or incidental information; they are not essential to the basic idea that the sentence is conveying.

Essential: The man who is sitting in that chair by the wall is our neighbor.

Nonessential: Our neighbor, who is sitting in that chair by the wall, is well-liked in our community.

Usage note: The only nonessential clause used at this level of *Editor in Chief*® is the appositive (a noun or noun/pronoun phrase, next to a noun, that identifies, defines, or explains the noun).

A sentence will not contain two dependent clauses without an independent clause.

To aid in remembering the rules for punctuating clauses, think of them as follows:

I + I = comma

I + D = no comma

D + I = comma

Note that the rules above apply to clauses, not phrases. For more on the difference between clauses and phrases, see pages 73–4.

Run-on Sentences

5.37   In this level of *Editor in Chief*®, the answer key corrects run-on sentences by creating two sentences: the first ending in a period and the second beginning with a capital letter. Although in the answers we do not provide all the alternatives listed below, you may wish to correct the run-on sentences using a semicolon or conjunction.

Incorrect: One sea lion balanced a ball another sea lion waved his flipper.

Incorrect: One sea lion balanced a ball, another sea lion waved his flipper.

Correct: One sea lion balanced a ball. Another sea lion waved his flipper.

Correct: One sea lion balanced a ball; another sea lion waved his flipper.

Correct: One sea lion balanced a ball, and another sea lion waved his flipper.

Sentence Fragments

5.38   In this level of *Editor in Chief*®, the answer key corrects sentence fragments by joining the sentence fragment to a complete sentence.

Incorrect: The bird was sitting on the roof. Sunning himself.

Correct: The bird was sitting on the roof sunning himself.

Note that a sentence fragment may also be corrected by rewriting the sentence in other ways, as shown below. We leave this to your discretion.

Possible: Sunning himself, the bird sat on the roof.

SPELLING

Homonyms...and other "Sound Alikes"

6.1   In this level of *Editor in Chief*®, we focus on the following homonyms:

are/our	to/too/two
in to/into	where/were
its/it's	whose/who's
lose/loose	your/you're
their/they're/there	week/weak

Plurals

6.2   Some words have the same form for the singular and plural.

sheep   deer   bison

6.3   The plurals of words that end in the sound of *f* are usually formed by changing the *f* to *v* and adding *-es*.

leaf/leaves   knife/knives

6.4   The plurals of words that end in *y* are usually formed by changing the *y* to *i* and adding *-es*.

berry/berries

Possessives

See "Apostrophe" on page 78.

Special Usage Problems

6.5   could of/could have: *could of* should not be used for *could have*; *of* should not be used for *have*

a lot: *a lot* is always two words

Note: Some words can be spelled in more than one way. For example, both of the following are correct:

toward   towards

READING DETECTIVE ™ B SAMPLE ACTIVITY

On the following pages is a sample activity from our popular reading series, *Reading Detective*™. There are currently three books in the series, *Beginning Reading Detective*, grades 3–4, *Reading Detective A1*, grades 5–6, and *Reading Detective B1*, grades 7–8. The following sample is from the Bl book.

- *Reading Detective*™ is based on national and state reading standards. These books, however, go beyond current reading comprehension materials by requiring 1) a higher level of analysis and 2) evidence to support answers. Students are asked to read a passage, then answer a variety of questions, supporting their answers with specific evidence from the passage. This skill, required by most state standards, is not often addressed in the available reading materials.

- Skills covered include basic reading skills such as reading for detail and identifying the main idea, literary analysis skills such as analyzing character traits and identifying setting, and critical thinking skills such as making inferences and distinguishing between cause and effect.

- Each book includes excerpts from works of award-winning authors and original fiction in a variety of genres: mystery, fantasy, adventure, humor. Nonfiction articles cover topics in science, social studies, math, and the arts that coincide with classroom curriculum.

- For further samples and information on the *Reading Detective*™ series, see our web site at www.CriticalThinking.com.

---

20. Old Woman of the Oak by Margaret Hockett

[1]I crossed the stream, wound my way through the bushes, and came to a clearing. [2]The oak sprawled before me.

[3]I pressed a dark knot on the pale gray trunk. [4]A rope ladder immediately snaked its way down through rustling red leaves. [5]A note had been tacked to the third rung: CAREFUL, JUDE. ROPE WET. [6]That was Old Meg, never one to waste words.

[7]Soon, I was swinging my legs into the entrance. [8]Meg sat in her "living room" in the oak she called home. [9]She was as gnarled as the tree, but her eyes usually crackled with fire. [10]Today they were flat.

[11]"Won't be much longer," she said. [12]"They're going to bulldoze the field for the new road."

[13]"No way!" I said in disbelief. [14]"We'll stop them—" [15]She held up her hand.

[16]"But where will you go…?" I started.

[17]She was moving her rocker back, baack, baaack—until it was on the edge of the runner and you thought she was going all the way over!—and then forward. [18]She'd do that when she was making up her mind.

[19]"Been here 'bout long enough. [20]Seen the sun set nine thousand times, and ain't none of them been the same as the one before." [21]I followed her gaze past dewy leaves, a patch of meadow, and jutting rocks of the coast. [22]An inky line was forming a boundary between sea and sky. [23]Suddenly, it spread, as if an artist were washing the scene with a dark tint. [24]My mood darkened with it as Meg's meaning came home to me.

[25]"I'm leaving you my Oak Log," she announced. [26]Her precious journal! [27]Meg thought the road project was a sign that her time had come, that her life was over! [28]I couldn't accept that.

[29]As I walked back to town, I ignored the slapping branches, the wet stream, and the cold night. [30]I was making a plan.

SAMPLE QUESTIONS

2. Paragraph B suggests that Meg's speech is
   A. brief.
   B. lengthy.
   C. mean.
   D. descriptive.

   Give the number of the sentence that best supports your answer. ____

3. In sentence 9, *gnarled* most likely means
   A. hard.
   B. twisted.
   C. tall.
   D. awesome.

6. Jude is most likely to make a plan to
   A. force Meg to move.
   B. move in with Meg.
   C. get the Oak Log.
   D. stop the bulldozing.

   List the numbers of the 2 sentences that best support your answer. ____, ____

10. In sentence 24, what does Jude infer from Meg's comments?

    _____

    _____

    _____

    Give the number of the sentence that confirms Jude's inference. ____

SAMPLE ANSWERS

2. Paragraph B suggests that Meg's speech is (character trait)
   A. brief.
   B. lengthy.
   C. mean.
   D. descriptive.

   1 best evidence sentence: **6**

3. In sentence 9, *gnarled* most likely means (vocabulary)
   A. hard.
   B. twisted.
   C. tall.
   D. awesome.

   Since *gnarled* is contrasted with the liveliness of her eyes, the author probably wants to show that Meg's body is aged, as a tree with knots and twisted branches.

6. Jude is most likely to make a plan to (predict outcome)
   A. force Meg to move.
   B. move in with Meg.
   C. get the Oak Log.
   D. stop the bulldozing.

   2 best evidence sentences: **13, 14**

   Choice D is supported by sentences 13 and 14, which show that Jude has strong feelings against the bulldozing. B is unlikely because there is no evidence that moving in with Meg would help. Since Meg is already going to give Jude the Oak Log, C is incorrect. A is a possibility but is unsupported.

10. In sentence 24, what does Jude infer from Meg's comments? (inference)

    He probably infers that Meg thinks her time has come to leave or die or both.

    1 best evidence sentence: **27**